SuperCharge Your Sales Force

APPLYING THE POWER OF COMPUTERS TO GET THE BEST FROM YOUR SALES TEAM

JON C. LIBERMAN

PROBUS PUBLISHING COMPANY
Chicago, Illinois
Cambridge, England

ISBN 1-55738-441-X
Printed in the United States of America

BB

1 2 3 4 5 6 7 8 9 0

CB/BJS

DEDICATION

I would like to thank Karen Liberman for her patience and support; David Epstein, Arnie Kimmel, and Monte Rifkin for their friendship and advice; Joe Pettit and David Hubanks for their professional feedback and critiques; and the professionals at Probus Publishing, without whom this book would never have been completed, for their assistance and writing skills. I also want to thank the software firms that are listed in the appendix of this book for their information and assistance.

CONTENTS

Chapter 1

INTRODUCTION

Selling is an integral part of any successful business. In fact, there are probably more salespeople in the United States than in any other single profession or means of employment. So it makes sense, given the spread of the information age and computing, to provide a concise, down-to-earth, non-computerese description of how to successfully automate salespeople.

That's what this book is all about.

The title of this book—*SuperCharge Your Sales Force*—suggests opportunities for salespeople and selling organizations to drastically improve their productivity and selling effectiveness.

This book provides both the theory and practical considerations of automating salespeople in today's business climate. The selling concepts elaborated are valuable in their own right, but when combined with the power of microcomputers, they provide a winning combination that will increase your bottom-line profitability.

SuperCharge Your Sales Force provides a step-by-step process for utilizing microcomputers to sell smarter and make more money.

The book has been written for salespeople, sales and marketing managers, and business owners in the following industries:

- Manufacturing Businesses. To get the most from your distribution channels—in-house sales and outside salespeople, independent sales reps, and distributors.

- Distributing businesses. To manage your sales staff and independent sales reps.

- Independent Sales Rep Organizations. To supercharge your salespeople's effectiveness.

- Service Organizations. To enhance your account executive/sales staff and consultants/professional selling results.

- Retail Operations. To improve your salespeople's client follow-up and personalized service selling.

- Telemarketing Organizations. To enhance your firm's phone effectiveness.

The concepts and techniques discussed in *SuperCharge Your Sales Force* apply equally to both telephone and field selling efforts. Management will benefit by learning how to assist the sales force in improving productivity and effectiveness, while increasing the synergy and continuity of marketing programs and efforts.

The following topics are discussed:

- Chapter 2: Why Automate the Sales Process?—Discover the potential benefits of implementing sales automation successfully in your business.

- Chapter 3: Managing the Sales Pipeline—Learn how to manage the assets of selling (people, time, and opportunities to do business).

- Chapter 4: The Numbers Game—How to Win at It!— Learn how to break your selling cycle (or sales pipeline) into targets or milestones to improve selling effectiveness over the long run.

- Chapter 5: Being in the Right Place at the Right Time— Learn the secrets of using computers to manage your follow-up efforts in order to ensure maximum sales results.

- Chapter 6: The Secrets of Making Time Work for You— Learn how to utilize automation to maximize your selling productivity.

- Chapter 7: Management's Perspective—Ensure management "covers all the bases" when considering implementing sales and contact management automation. The old adage, "an ounce of prevention is worth a pound of cure," has never been more relevant than when applied to automating business.

- Chapter 8: Determining What to Automate—Learn how to determine what to automate in your sales process. We will incorporate the computer software requirements discussed in the previous chapters into your personal requirements list.

- Chapter 9: How to Evaluate and Select Sales Management Software—Learn how to compare your personal requirements list to packaged software systems and vendors to discover how to pick the right system for you.

- Chapter 10: What Not to Do!—Learn from common mistakes other businesses and salespeople have made when attempting to automate.

- Chapter 11: Conclusions—Summary of what we have covered and how you can use this book to sell smarter!

At the end of Chapters 3 through 7 a Case Study provides real-life illustrations of the topics discussed. Also at the end of these chapters is a Software Features Checklist that lists the features and functions you need in sales management software to utilize the topics discussed in the chapter. This checklist will help you determine the exact requirements for your sales and contact management system.

Chapters 8 through 10 discuss the practical aspects of selecting and implementing a software system for your own use.

Chapter 9 contains a sample requirements checklist. This information will be invaluable in helping you determine your own system requirements as well as selecting a software package to meet your needs. Critiques of 10 of the most popular PC-based sales management and contact management systems are also included in the Appendix (comparison of requirements checklist and 10 software packages) as well as information on the 10 products evaluated.

First of all, let's cover the basics.

What Is a Computer System?

Before you attempt to computerize your business or yourself, it is important to understand what a computer is—from a practical perspective.

A computer is basically a calculator, typewriter, and filing cabinet combined. Whatever you can do with a calculator, typewriter, and filing cabinet, you can do with a computer system—nothing magical, nothing more—although a computer can process the work much faster than you and will make fewer mistakes. If you want to know if a computer can do a particular job, ask yourself: Could I do it with the above tools and time? (See Figure 1–1)

How to Use the Software Features Checklist

We elaborate on how to use computers to sell smarter in Chapters 3 through 7. At the end of each chapter we list the specific features you need in a software system to effectively implement the theories and concepts discussed. As you review this information, determine for yourself which features will be valuable to you. In

Figure 1-1 What Is a Computer?

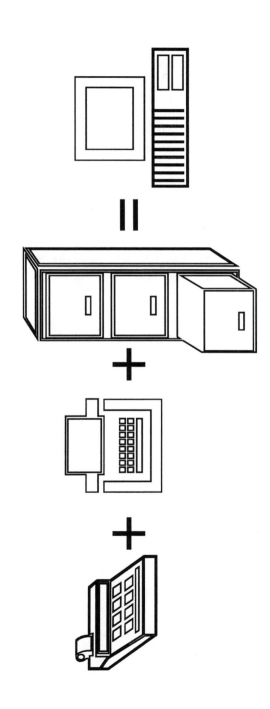

Chapter 8 we discuss how to determine what to automate, so you can tie all your critical needs and wants together in an organized manner.

By determining your system requirements and comparing them to the packages critiqued (or any other package you are aware of), you can make an intelligent and informed decision as to the best alternatives available to you and your firm.

Chapter 2

WHY AUTOMATE THE SALES PROCESS?

One of the first questions a salesperson or manager should ask is Why? *Why should I bother automating in the first place?*

Do the following scenarios remind you of anyone you know?

Scenario 1

Your secretary pages you to let you know Mr. Thompson is returning your call; you're certain he was one of those cold calls you just made—one where you left a message; you scramble to locate the index card where you have all the information on your previous conversation. You hope you can find it in time to avoid the certain embarrassment you will feel if you can't remember who the guy is before you pick up the phone.

The Solution . . .

If you had a sales and contact management software system and microcomputer on your desk, you could immediately locate Mr. Thompson by typing his name in the quick search field (or similar function in any contact management system) and scrolling through the database until the appropriate "Mr. Thompson" came up on your screen. A simple review of your personal notes would remind you who the gentleman is while you pick up the phone and say, "Mr. Thompson, thank you for returning my call, the reason for my call is . . ."

Scenario 2

As you hang up the phone, anguish overcomes you. If only you would have remembered to call them back last month. You were certain they would call you when the board of directors finally okayed the funds. After all, the board had held up the decision for over six months. But your competitor was in front of them at the right time and place and closed the deal before you could get back in the door.

The Solution . . .

If you used a sales and contact management software system, you would have had the prospect on a regular follow-up program. The computer would have reminded you daily of the calls you needed to make and the tasks you needed to accomplish. You would have called the account a month ago and at least had a shot at the business.

Scenario 3

Last quarter you were riding high. Your region had the highest sales of any in the country. You can't understand what happened. This quarter looks like the bottom is falling out. Your salespeople's projections were way off the mark. How can you get out of this feast or famine cycle?

The Solution . . .

If you and your sales staff were using a sales management system and managing your sales pipeline effectively (as elaborated in Chapter 3), you would have known months in advance that you were going to have a problem—known in time to do something about it. Contact management systems that provide the means to manage your sales cycles and perform sales projections can help minimize the feast and famine cycles so common in today's marketplace.

Why should you bother automating? The answer is simple. Using automation wisely improves your productivity and decision-making abilities and will help you make more sales. In essence it can help you work smarter!

Benefits of Sales Automation

Sales management will receive the following benefits from automating the sales force:

- Salespeople will get help in improving their productivity and sales effectiveness.

- The sales staff won't have to spend as much time and effort producing all the required management reports.

- Using direct-mail and telemarketing campaigns for targeted markets will improve marketing effectiveness.

- Management will have more control over sales staff and corporate assets in the form of prospect and client databases.

- Ability to analyze return on market investments will improve.

- Management decision-making and reporting will improve.

- Communication between management and sales staff will improve.

More Productive Time

The more time salespeople can spend selling, as opposed to administrating, the more sales they can make. Sales software can minimize paperwork and administrative time by automating the sales process and management reporting requirements. You can input prospect, sales, or agenda information once, and have it available whenever you need it—on the screen or printed out—or you can download information over the phone to your office.

Sales management systems can provide productivity improvements for salespeople by automating the following functions:

- *Management Reporting.* Provide management with activity tracking, sales projections, account profiles, and other required reports.

- *Database Inquiry.* Database tools that enable quick access to information. Eliminate wasted time looking for client names, notes, and other important information.

- *Agenda Management Capabilities.* Enable quick entry and update of scheduled events (phone calls, tasks, meetings, etc.).

- *Computerized Communications.* Provide the ability to send and receive information over the phone, to send management reporting requests to your home office via modems, to send quotes or proposals to your clients via computer faxes, or to hook up to your central computer to send/receive messages, etc.

Access to More Information

This is especially true in the sales process. Sales management systems can provide the facts you need, at the touch of a button. You can track important information on prospects and customers, demographic information, sales cycles, hot buttons, "user profiles," marketing plan effectiveness, and other relevant information.

Having the information you need, when you need it, often makes the difference between a sale and an excuse. Most contact management systems enable you to define certain fields of information as "user-defined" (which means you can capture information that *you* determine is important that otherwise is not "built into" the database). This allows you to capture information on each account that is unique to your business. For instance, the specific products or services the account is interested in, who your competition is, how large the account is, when the boss's birthday is, and so on. Other critical information you should track is the source of the lead (to track marketing effectiveness), the business type, what information you have sent them, personal notes on your discussions, where they are in the sales cycle, and so on.

To determine what information would be valuable for you to keep track of, answer the following questions:

- Who do you sell to ? Are your targeted markets based on industry, geographic location, size of business, types of products/services they purchase?

- What information do you need to know about your targeted market prospects to effectively locate and qualify them?

- What information would be useful when evaluating whether or not you should spend money (resources) on a particular marketing program (for instance, attending a particular trade show, or advertising in a newspaper, investing in a mailing campaign, or using a particular telemarketing firm)?

- What information, if you had access to it on demand, would enable you to close more business (information such as account budgeting cycles, decision makers, problems they are experiencing, old technology they are using, and so on)?

Being at the Right Place at the Right Time

Being at the right place at the right time is seen as luck to many novices. Sales professionals know they make their own luck. Keeping in touch with prospects and clients on a regular basis maximizes your opportunity to be at the right place at the right time.

Automation can eliminate scraps of paper, memory lapses, prospects "falling through the cracks," and missed opportunities. Sales management systems can automate your callbacks, calendar, "to-do" lists, and other items requiring timely attention.

Once you have determined a particular account is a good prospect for your firm, using a computerized follow-up system will give you tremendous advantages over manual systems by allowing you to do the following:

- Automate daily call and to-do lists to ensure you do not forget any important calls or tasks.

- Keep on top by scheduling events (calls, meetings, tasks, etc.) once—when programmed, the system will remind you of what you need to do. Some systems actually provide audio alarms.

- Access account information with the touch of a button. Locate prospects using your own criteria (particular product interest, geographic location, and so on) and remember whatever details of previous conversations you feel are important by reviewing your free-form notepad.

- Create detailed history on each account by simply using the sales management system. As you record completed tasks, phone calls, and so on, the system automatically records your activities.

Personal Touch

Providing that "personal touch" that makes your clients feel special is a key ingredient to successful, long-term business relationships.

Free-form notepads can provide you instant access to personal notes on each client so you never forget those important details. Many systems automatically date and user-stamp each entry, so you can keep track of every conversation and memo regarding the account. This feature of contact management systems provides tremendous benefits for those sales professionals who value building a relationship with their clients.

In addition to free-form notepads, sales management systems allow you to easily track important client dates, such as birthdays and anniversaries, enabling you to get cards or personal notes out on time. Retail salespeople can also use sales management software to provide that personal touch to their top clients by tracking client preferences, sizes, and so on. For instance, when a new shipment of suits comes in, you can easily locate those clients who would be interested.

Telemarketing and Direct Mail

Automate the telemarketing and direct-mail processes to more productively generate qualified leads. Computerized telemarketing scripts can improve telemarketers' effectiveness. Direct-mailing systems can pinpoint qualified prospects based upon demographic, geographic, industry, or other criteria.

Sales management systems make creating your own client/prospect database an easy reality. Target marketing—integrating direct-mail and telemarketing campaigns—will provide high volume and quality leads. Management can particularly benefit by ensuring a consistent message when using automated scripts and tracking salesperson or promotional program effectiveness with minimal effort.

Businesses spend millions of dollars every year on purchasing various mailing lists. Developing your own database of potential clients will provide a valuable asset to your business. Sales management systems give you the wherewithal to create accurate, useful databases that improve over time.

Improve Sales Management Control

Sales management can benefit by improved control over the sales system and lead-tracking activities. Automated sales tracking systems and prospect databases, including free-form notepads and sales history, allow management to know what's going on with any client or prospect.

The sales continuity that management will receive by automating all salespeople into one corporate database is a critical benefit. Without effective systems, when a salesperson leaves your employment, you lose most of the accounts she or he has been working. The time and energy to "re-create" their accounts wastes valuable resources; or, new salespeople simply have to start over. In either case, when properly implemented and used, sales management systems will ensure continuity of all your sales efforts.

Better Analyze Your Return on Market Investments

Improve your ability to evaluate the effectiveness of your marketing efforts and investments by tracking lead sources and marketing campaign results. Sales management systems can provide concrete information on the return on investment (ROI) of your marketing dollars. Take the guesswork out of your marketing investments.

Knowing where your business comes from is a critical factor in any effective marketing plan. Being in the position to track, on an on-going basis, where your leads are generated from and the percentages that convert into clients is difficult with manual systems. Sales management systems can provide sales and marketing management with the facts they need to effectively target the best means of generating quality leads.

Improve Management Decision-Making

Improve management decision-making by providing timely, accurate information on customers, sales staff, product penetration, marketing campaigns, and so on. Customized reporting is available to provide insight into many aspects of the marketing and sales efforts.

Business decisions are typically only as good as the information they are based upon. Accuracy and timeliness are the cornerstones of effective and useful information. The difficulties of capturing accurate information and having it available on a timely basis with manual systems is evident to anyone who has attempted to do so. Automated sales management systems will simplify the capturing of information and allow on-demand reporting.

Typical reports generated from sales management systems include the following:

- Detailed summary activity reporting by salespeople.

- Projected sales for period (user defined) by salespeople.

- Marketing plan (or mailing list) members.

- Source of leads reports.

- Sales pipeline or sales cycle reports.

- Standard Industry Classification (SIC) code or business type lists.

- Account profiles (lists all information on a range of accounts).

- User-defined and *ad hoc* reports created on demand. These reports typically can be based upon any information you have defined in your database.

- Various agenda reports by salespeople for a range of dates.

Improve Communication

Improve communication between your management and sales staff by using electronic mail and telecommunications via laptop computers in the field.

Communications between staff who are involved in selling and servicing clients is critical to maintaining high customer service levels. This is especially true for situations involving outside salespeople and inside customer service representatives. Sales management systems typically allow for sharing of information on networks and/or downloading information from remote computers (such as laptops) to a central office system via modems over the phone line.

Critical information to share can include agenda and calendar schedules, electronic notepads, to-do lists and activities to follow up on, electronic memos, sales orders, and management reporting requests.

Any selling involving multiple contacts, on-going business relationships between the client and sales force, or heavy reliance on the use of the phone or telemarketing can benefit as outlined above.

Practicing What You Preach

I owned a microcomputer consulting practice for eight years. We were the typical, under-capitalized, start-up operation. We grew to 21 associates through hard work, personal sacrifice, and being in a growth industry (early 1980s). The problem was, I was spread too thin, having to be everything to everybody. I was working 60-plus hours a week, and was stressed out and underpaid. When my wife got pregnant with our first child, I decided this was not what I wanted my life to be like.

After evaluating our options, we decided to pursue a merger with a mid-sized CPA firm. We approached several firms and received three offers. After completing the negotiations with the selected firm, my personal goals were to focus on doing the things I enjoyed the most. Handling, selling, and doing the front-end consulting were the most profitable and allowed me time to spend with my family.

In my new position, my first task was to be able finally to practice what I preached. I was selling computer systems, improved productivity, and the like, but never had the time to automate myself. I evaluated the marketplace and selected a contact management software package. This book is based on my experience, and the experience of others who took the plunge and organized themselves around microcomputers.

Approximately 18 months after implementing the software, I have more than doubled my income (and continue to increase it), while working fewer hours (40–45 a week, including the administration time of working in a CPA firm). My success story is not unique. Many sales professionals have had similar success. The ingredients of success are:

1. Have a clear picture in your mind of what you are going to accomplish; you need specific measurable targets and to be focused on achieving them.

2. Select a software/hardware solution that meets your requirements and is easy to use. (I will cover how to determine your needs and pick the appropriate software throughout this book.)

3. Institute the personal disciplines required to use the software. This last item is the most critical and where most attempts to automate fail. You must use the tools every working day to get the payback.

As a salesperson, I look at a computer as a tool to help me be more productive. One of the key advantages of sales management systems is their ability to help you manage your sales process to guarantee success.

Summary

The following are benefits of sales management systems:

1. *More productive time.* The more time salespeople can spend selling as opposed to administering, the more sales they can make.

2. *Information is power.* Sales management systems can provide the facts you need at the touch of a button.

3. *Being in the right place at the right time.* Being at the right place at the right time is seen as luck to many novices. Sales professionals know they make their own luck. Keeping in touch with prospects and clients on a regular basis maximizes your opportunity to be at the right place at the right time.

4. *Personal touch.* Providing the personal touch that makes your clients feel special is a key ingredient to successful, long-term sales relationships.

5. *Telemarketing and direct mail.* Automate the telemarketing and direct mail processes to more productively generate qualified leads.

6. *Improved sales management control.* Sales management can benefit by improved control over the sales staff and lead-tracking activities. Automated systems can provide continuity to your sales system.

7. *Improved analysis of return on marketing investment.* Improve your ability to evaluate the effectiveness of your marketing efforts and investments by tracking lead sources and marketing campaign results.

8. *Improved management decision-making.* Improve management decision-making by providing timely, accurate information on customers, sales staff, product penetration, marketing campaigns, and so on. Customized reporting is available to provide insight into many aspects of the marketing and sales efforts.

9. *Improved communication.* Improve communication between your management and sales staff by using electronic mail and telecommunications via laptop computers in the field.

Chapter 3

MANAGING THE SALES PIPELINE TO GUARANTEE SUCCESS!

What Business Are You in?

Asking the question above may seem simplistic or foolish, but it is the first step in figuring out how to use a computer to make more money. I am assuming that a major aspect of your day-to-day work involves either selling something to somebody or managing people who sell.

If this is true, ultimately the business you are in is selling!

If you take the perspective that you are in the business of selling, and you look at the resources of selling as assets of your

---

business, you can gain a unique appreciation of how to better manage these resources to improve productivity.

How to Use Computers to Better Manage the Assets of Selling and Improve Profits

The assets of selling involve people (sales staff, support staff, management, etc.), the time spent (or invested) by these people, and the opportunities to do business (OTDBs) that exist in your marketplace (businesses that potentially can buy your product/service).

The focus of this book concerns the business of selling. To become more productive at selling, you must understand how to manage time more effectively and how to focus your efforts in the areas where you can receive the highest return on investment (ROI).

Manage Time More Effectively

Sales management systems can help you manage your time more effectively by providing the following capabilities:

- Agenda management functions keep track of all your calls and tasks and provide daily to-do lists to ensure you do not forget anything.

- Automated mailing functions can easily send personalized letters or form letters to an OTDB or a group of OTDBs.

- Fast-find and inquiry capabilities can locate specific clients, OTDBs, referral sources, etc., immediately, without wasting time.

- Sales management systems can create the administrative reports management wants by hitting one key. Salespeople can download over the phone or print out the information management wants, such as:

- Activity reports for a period of time

- Sales projections

- Lead source reports

- Booked orders reports

- Expense reports

- Other sales-related information

Manage Your OTDBs to Maximize Your ROI

Every business considers the money owed to it a critical asset of the corporation. Accounts receivables are therefore carefully managed to ensure minimal write-offs and bad debts. It is amazing that many businesses do not treat their OTDBs with as much consideration or care. The OTDBs in your marketplace are the potentials for generating sales.

The prospect and customer database that a company creates and sells to is a valuable asset of the business that needs to be managed as carefully as the money owed to it. To understand how to use computers to better manage the OTDBs of a business, one must understand the sales process.

The sales process is, in some ways, the most critical process of any business enterprise. Nothing happens that generates money until the sale is made (the deal is closed). It is essential that you understand the process or cycle you follow when selling.

Traditional Selling Cycle (Process)

1. *Suspect Stage*: Most sales start at the suspect stage. This is the initial stage of qualifying. You have a rough idea that a particular business or individual may fit the model of someone (or some business) who would buy your product/service. You probably have never spoken to this account, but they seem to have the characteristics of a viable prospect.

In essence, a suspect is someone worth calling on to discover if they're a good fit with what you sell.

2. *Prospect Qualifying Stage*: A prospect is a suspect with whom you have made contact, and with whom the initial response seems favorable. Or at least you could hypothesize that they may want your product/service at a future date.

   In the Prospect Qualifying Stage you are asking questions to determine the following qualifiers:

   - How will the decision to buy be made, and by whom? Where in the buying cycle is this prospect?

   - Does the prospect have *bona fide* needs that my firm can satisfy?

   - Can the prospect afford the solution to their problem?

   - Is there any urgency to act now or in the near future?

   Once you have established that the prospect meets your qualifications, move to the next stage.

3. *Developing the Solution Stage*: In this stage you are helping prospects define their needs in such a way as to fit your product/service. Your goal at this stage is to understand what "wins" the decision-makers require, both from their own personal perspective and that of their firm (I'm assuming non-consumer sales).

   Effective questioning is the typical tool of this stage. You need to understand what problems, needs, and objectives your prospect has, so you can relate the benefits of your product/service to the prospect's requirements. In essence, in the Developing Solution Stage you are determining what solution your prospect requires and how your product/services can satisfy that need.

4. *Presenting Your Solution Stage*: Once you have defined the prospect's needs and have gained agreement from the

prospect on what they are committed to do, you can move into the next stage, which involves presenting your firm and product/service to the prospect in such a way as to create confidence in your solution and a desire to own your solution.

Demonstrating your product and presenting proposals, sales presentations, and other similar activities make up the nuts and bolts of this stage. The objective of this process is to position both your firm and your solution in the mind of the prospect as uniquely qualified to satisfy their needs.

5. *Closing the Deal Stage*: As the name suggests, closing the deal is where the commissions are earned, the commitment to buy is received, and the prospect becomes a customer.

6. *Keeping the Business Stage*: Most sales endeavors attempt to create an ongoing relationship with the client. Repeat business opportunities and referrals are important components to most business prosperity.

The objective of this stage is to keep clients happy with your firm and product/service so that they will be inclined to do business with you on an ongoing basis. Any sales professional recognizes that reselling to happy customers provides a better return on their investment (in time) than having to create new relationships with first-time clients.

The business you are in may have unique or different variables or factors, but in any selling situation managing the sales process effectively is a key ingredient to continued success.

The Sales Pipeline

One useful way to look at the process, and to understand how automating it can improve your productivity (better manage the assets), is to compare the sales cycle to a pipeline (Figure 3–1).

Figure 3–1 Sales Pipeline Management

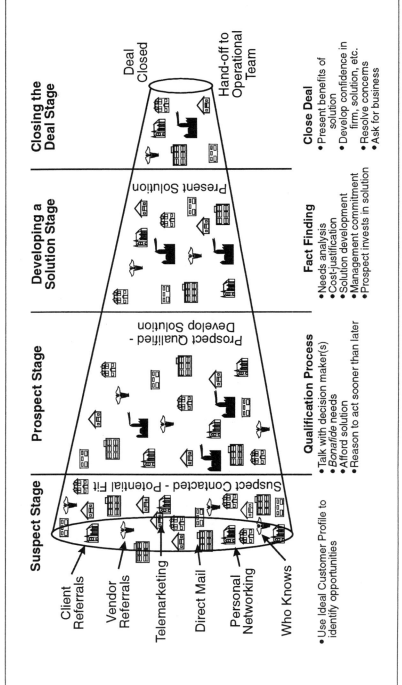

The sales pipeline can provide insight and means of managing the OTDBs of your business.

On the far left of your sales pipeline is the Suspects Stage; as you contact them and begin qualifying them, they move to the right of the pipeline, into the Prospect Qualifying Stage; as you work the prospects, they either move to the right—throughout your sales process until you close them—or they are discarded and taken out of the process (pipeline). You notice in the above diagram that the pipeline opens widely, then progressively narrows. This represents the fact that the number of prospects you start the process with tends to diminish and that you close only a percentage of them.

The secret to managing the sales pipeline is to ensure that the two ends are full. Focus on closing your hot prospects, at the far right of the pipeline (Close The Deal Stage) and on feeding new suspects/prospects into the far left (Suspect Stage).

This is CRITICAL! You must be feeding new suspects into your Sales Pipeline continually to ensure consistent revenue and to maximize your productivity.

Staying out of the Feast or Famine Cycle

Have you ever noticed the tendency for your sales (and commissions) to go through cycles? You work hard to get a large contract, focusing all your efforts on it, at the cost of prospecting. You close the deal, earn large commissions, and then the following months you scramble to find another deal, while your earnings suffer. Managing your sales pipeline can eliminate (or minimize) this common cycle.

There are six key steps involved in managing the sales pipeline:

1. Determine the numbers/targets you need to achieve. A critical component of managing anything is being able to measure and quantify what it is you are attempting to accomplish. You must establish goals that your sales pipeline can measure (described in detail in Chapter 4).

One of the critical numbers you need to determine is how many suspects you need in order to generate the number of sales required within your targeted time frame.

2. Determine how you will "feed the pipeline." For each market segment you are selling to, you need to determine how you will generate leads. Various promotional and lead-generating activities can be used (telemarketing, direct mail, seminars, trade shows, advertising, etc.).

3. Determine your "Ideal Customer Profile." You need to determine, for each product line or service area you sell, what the ideal customer looks like. This Ideal Customer Profile is used to determine who should be "fed" into your sales pipeline and what the qualification characteristics are (described in detail in Chapter 5).

4. Determine the appropriate follow-up programs necessary for each product/service line and market segment. We will discuss in Chapter 5 how to be at the right place at the right time with prospects and customers. One critical component of this is to determine how often and via what media (phone call, mail, etc.) you need to keep in contact with an OTDB.

5. Determine, for each product/service line and market segment, what has to occur to move the account to the next stage in the sales pipeline. For instance, when selling life insurance, once you have determined that a prospect is about to have their first child, they may move from the Prospect Qualifying Stage to the Developing a Solution Stage. You know that people begin to think about life insurance when they begin a family; they therefore are qualified (assuming they have any money) and should be pursued more aggressively.

6. Determine how to monitor and evaluate the success of your marketing programs, follow-up programs, and sales techniques. Once you have established numbers/targets to reach for, you can track your actual ver-

sus targeted results. This step allows for fine-tuning and feedback on what you are doing to manage your sales pipeline and gives you the opportunity to enhance your effectiveness. You'd be amazed at how infrequently some people evaluate the effectiveness of what they're doing. You need to determine what information you need to keep track of in order to keep yourself on target. (For elaboration, see the Case Study at the end of this chapter.)

When you follow these six steps, you will be in a position to proactively manage the sales process. You will not be surprised that sales have fallen off projections (you will see it coming months in advance and have a chance to do something about it); you will understand what kind of efforts will be required to meet targets (because you are tracking your numbers and the progress of your OTDBs in the pipeline); and you will be able to evaluate accurately the effectiveness of your marketing investment and sales skills (by tracking revenue by lead source and evaluating where your OTDBs in the pipeline are stuck).

How Computers Help You Manage Your Sales Pipeline

Contact management software can easily provide the means of tracking each prospect in your sales cycle. Each prospect in your database can contain a field of information that tracks a progress level or step in the sales cycle. You need the software to request an update of this field every time you record an activity as completed in your contact management system. (An activity may be a phone call, a letter, a meeting, or a task completion.) Pop-up windows containing your sales pipeline steps should be visible, simplifying the updating process (Figure 3–2).

Once you have accurately classified your prospects in this manner, your software should provide reports (or screen inquiries) totaling the number of contacts by sales pipeline step. These pipeline management reports should be available by various sorting criteria (i.e., for a particular product line or marketing plan). You can compare the number of contacts targeted in each step

Figure 3-2 Pop-Up Window with Sales Pipeline Steps

```
TRACK
Contact  Results  Task  DoneTask  NextDate  Failed  Progress  ViewHistory  Quit
Update progress code

Company Interactive                        Phone        Ext       Time/Date
Contact John Overend                       (708) 490-9600         10:08A L
Title   VP                                 (800) 451-1646         06/15/93
Dear:   John
Address 2401 Hassell rd                    AcctExec Jon C. Liberman
        Suite 1500                         Bus
City    Hoffman Estates      State IL      Pro 0 - Suspect
Country USA           Zip 60195            Rat 1 - Initial Contact
Source  Personal/JCL                       Pot 2 - Qualifying
                                               3 - Fact Finding
                                               4 - Proposal
                                           Next 5 - Presentation/Demo
                                           When 6 - Ask to buy
                                           Next 7 - Active Client Project
                                           Prior 8 - Client - new opportunity
                                               9 - Inactive Client
                                           Next
TRACKING                                   When Due    /  /     12:00P
Last Contact   Call                        Priority
When Completed 06/14/93  2:28P  :
Last Objective F/U Musikantow AST
Results        Completed

Last Attempt      /  /      12:00A
Reason Failed

                    DY-Select  Backspace-Clear
```

M
D

with your actual numbers to determine if any corrective action must be taken to manage your pipeline (Figure 3–3).

Case Study: Managing the Sales Process

In the previous chapter's Case Study, I discussed the success I have achieved by using microcomputers to improve my selling productivity and effectiveness. I will now elaborate on how I use microcomputers to manage the assets of my business for a selected product line.

1. The first step was for me to set targets for myself. I selected a long-term (3–5 years) income goal and worked backwards to determine what I needed to earn each year to reach my goal. (Obviously, if you don't set realistic goals, you're only fooling yourself; on the other hand, you want to pick targets that make you stretch.)

2. Next, I selected several "product lines" to sell that my firm could deliver and that would provide real value to my clients. For the sake of this case study, I will discuss one product line—a packaged software system written for distributors, manufacturers, and financial management. The product I selected provides several competitive advantages, but I will not elaborate on them here. I needed to sell a product/service that I believed in, that was competitive, and that satisfied the users' (customers') needs. I selected this product line (as part of my firm's market planning) because of its high profitability and ability to create repeat business opportunities.

3. I estimated what the typical sale would generate in terms of fees, product profits, and commissions. I determined what an optimistic goal would be in terms of the number and size of the sales I could close over a year.

4. I established standards (based on my experience) on the following items: the number of prospects to whom I

Figure 3-3   Sample Pipeline Report

PROGRESS COUNTS

Report Date: June 15, 1993

Progress Level	Count	Average Rating	Potential Sale	Calculated Proj. Sale
0 – Suspect	1	0.0	0.00	0.00
1 – Initial Contact	1	0.0	0.00	0.00
2 – Qualifying	22	0.0	0.00	0.00
5 – Presentation/Dem	3	27.7	205,000.00	56,716.67
6 – Ask to buy	2	20.0	75,000.00	15,000.00
7 – Active Client Pr	6	0.0	0.00	0.00
8 – Client – new opp	1	0.0	0.00	0.00
9 – Inactive Client	2	0.0	0.00	0.00
99 – Dead	2	0.0	0.00	0.00
A – Not Qualified	7	0.0	0.00	0.00
B – Lost Deal	3	0.0	0.00	0.00
F – Telemarketing F/	9	0.0	0.00	0.00
	----	----	------------	---------
Grand Total	59	2.1	280,000.00	71,716.67
	====	====	============	=========

would have to provide a proposal and demonstrate the process before I would sell one system; the number of prospects I would have to qualify to present one proposal and demonstrate my product; and the number of suspects I would need to talk to to generate one viable prospect. (This process is described in detail in the Case Study in Chapter 4.) Based upon these estimates, I determined the effort required to reach my income goals. This process established the targets I needed to reach.

5. I investigated my target markets (Chicago-based manufacturers, distributors, and high-growth, mid-sized businesses) to determine what lists and lead sources were available and which promotional activities we could implement that would feed my sales pipeline for this product line.

6. I developed an Ideal Customer Profile for my targeted market and used it to help screen suspects and qualify prospects. The Ideal Customer Profile also provided me with ideas on how to find viable prospects for my product line (described in Chapter 5).

7. I targeted several software vendors and consultants (who could refer me accounts) and set them up in my follow-up system to contact monthly for referrals. I also developed several form letters and created the means of easily sending information to qualified prospects about my firm and product line. Any product or service has its own lists, lead sources, and activities that generally can provide OTDBs. The key is to develop an action plan and then to use the computer to ensure prompt and efficient follow-up.

8. I established follow-up programs for each stage of my sales pipeline that ensured I would keep in front of the right prospects at the right time. Because of the nature of what I was selling—the sales cycle tends to be long (six-plus months) and multiple people are involved in

the decision-making process—I wanted to make sure that I knew who the players were, the time frames the client needed to act in, and their rationale for investigating (or planning to investigate) a new business computer system. I documented this information in my contact management system and determined how often (and when) I should next contact them.

If used properly, his process is the *heart and soul* of computer-aided productivity improvement. With minimal effort (I had to make the phone calls, ask pertinent questions, and input the information into my system), I was able to determine who I should keep in contact with and to implement a follow-up system that eliminated the need for me to remember anything. I simply retrieved my call list each day and made sure all my calls were made. I had all the pertinent information at my fingertips, and many prospects were impressed with my promptness and thoroughness.

Many of the calls lasted only five minutes—the prospect would tell me what had occurred since our last discussion and when I should follow up on them in the future. Once the prospect was qualified and moved into the Developing the Solution Stage, I would schedule a meeting, bring in my associates, and go through the process we'd established to develop the proposal, demonstrate the software, and so on. I didn't waste time with unqualified prospects.

9. It is important to remember that you need to constantly be feeding new suspects (referrals, etc.) into your sales pipeline. An effective software system will allow you to prioritize the calls scheduled each day, ensuring that you contact your hot prospects while continuing to qualify new suspects into prospects.

10. On a regular basis (monthly) I produced several reports that allowed me to track my progress and focus my efforts in the most profitable areas:

    - I looked at reports that contained the number of accounts I was working on in each stage of my sales pipeline. This let me know how I was doing based on my targets and standards (#4 above). If I was low in a particular stage, I could do something to improve the situation before it became a crisis.

    - I looked at my projected sales report (the Closing the Deal Stage). This projected what was estimated to close over the next 90 days so I could focus my efforts and manage the account to fruition (the deal closed).

    - I looked at several lead source reports that told me where my clients originated, what sources were most productive in the last 30–90 days (remember the sales cycle was typically over six months long), and where I should continue spending my effort (and money) generating leads.

    - Finally, I looked at profitability reports that showed me actual revenue by account and percentage of revenue for this product line. I wanted to ensure that the assumptions I'd made at the earlier steps concerning commissions and standards were accurate so that I could adapt them as required to ensure my goals were reached.

An additional benefit of this approach is that it allowed me to proactively find opportunities when something in my marketplace changed. For instance, when a major minicomputer manufacturer filed for bankruptcy, I was able—with minimal effort—to locate and contact all the prospects who presently had that manufacturer's computer. (I had categorized the type of computer they presently had in my database.) Also, when prospects I hadn't talked to in a while (or whose names I didn't remember) would call me, I was able to instantly find them in my database without rummaging through files, index cards, or the like. This saved me countless hours and embarrassments.

Summary

Before we list the software features and functions needed to utilize the concepts elaborated in the previous chapters, let's review what we have learned.

1. Salespeople can use computers to sell smarter, which translates into making more money in less time. In other words, supercharge your selling by doing the following:

    *   Have a clear picture in your mind of what you are going to accomplish; you need specific measurable targets and the focus to achieve them.

    *   Select a software/hardware solution that meets your requirements and is easy to use (covered in Chapters 8 and 9).

    *   Institute the personal disciplines required to use the software. This last item is the most critical and where most attempts to automate fail. You must use the tools every working day to get the payback.

2. To become more productive at selling, you must understand how to manage time more effectively, how to focus your efforts in the areas where you can receive the highest return on investment, and how to keep in front of the right OTDBs (Opportunities To Do Business) at the right time.

3. The secret to managing the sales pipeline is to insure that the two ends are full. Focus on closing your hot prospects at the far right of the pipeline (Closing the Deal Stage) and in feeding new suspects/prospects into the far left

(Suspect Stage). **This is CRITICAL!** You must be feeding new suspects continually into your sales pipeline to ensure consistent revenue and to maximize your productivity.

Software Features Checklist

To successfully utilize a computer system to manage your sales pipeline, the following features are necessary:

1. Progress level or sales cycle updated automatically when recording activity completion (phone call, letter, meeting, task).

   A critical requirement of managing your sales pipeline is categorizing, where each prospect in your pipeline is in your selling cycle (sales pipeline). In order to accommodate data accuracy, I suggest the progress level (or sales cycle) be a required update field upon completion of any sales activity (phone call, meeting, letter, task), thereby ensuring ease and accuracy of use.

   Most salespeople will not take the time to update a progress or sales cycle field unless they are forced to or the system makes it very easy to do so. If the data is inaccurate in your sales pipeline, it will be worse than useless.

   Required Software Functions:

   • Progress level or sales cycle field in contact database.

   • An update of the Progress/Sales field every time an activity is completed (referred to as a "required field" for data input).

   • Pop-up windows containing your sales pipeline steps to assist in data entry accuracy when inputting progress/sales cycle field.

- Report showing number of contacts per sales pipe-line step, with sorting available via user-selected criteria (market plan, business type, hot button, etc.).

2. Sales projections available on demand.

   Most companies request some sort of sales projection from their salespeople on a regular basis (quarterly, etc.). The companies are trying to get a handle on what the anticipated sales and revenues will be for the next time period. Most projections tend to be "guesstimates" at best, and are rarely accurate. When you use projections in conjunction with sales pipeline management techniques, you can accomplish these objectives:

   - Improving the accuracy of sales projections because you are actively managing and tracking the progress of each OTDB in your sales pipeline. When you track sales in this manner, you gain improved insights on what works, and what doesn't, in regard to closing business.

   - Measuring actual versus estimated (or projected) revenues.

   Required Software Functions:

   - Potential sale amount, target date, and rating (percentage of certainty) fields in the contact database.

   - Sales projection report sorted within range of dates and by salesperson.

   - **OPTIONAL:** You may require additional information (e.g., product line, territory, etc.) to create meaningful reports. You may be able to use user-defined fields to capture this information and then create the report using the system's ad hoc reporting capabilities.

3. Free-form notes to track personalized information on each contact.

The capability to record free-form notes for each contact is a critical requirement of any contact management system. These notes can be used to refresh your memory prior to a conversation with a prospect/client. The ability to remember details of conversations, to record commitments or comments, or to leave yourself notes will produce rewards. The ability to keep in contact with a large number of contacts, and be in a position to personalize your sales approach by using these free-form notes fields is a key component to effectively managing your sales pipeline.

If multiple people interact with a prospect or client, the ability to record all conversations and commitments in one place can be invaluable. Your knowing who said what to whom, when, gives your prospect the impression that your firm is organized and that you work together well.

Many sales management systems will automatically date and user-stamp each note entry. This stamp tells you when the note was recorded, and by whom.

Required Software Functions:

- Free-form notes fields available through window.

- The computer automatically puts into the notes field the date, time of day, and operator (or salesperson) who logged onto the system.

- **OPTIONAL:** You may want word search capabilities in your notes field. This allow you to locate occurrences where specific words are recorded in your notes field database.

4. Ability to import databases of prospects into system.

Required Software Functions:

- Import capability in system via diskette or modem. The system must allow for defining the type of file to be read (e.g., ASCII, DIF, etc.).

- The system must allow you to define the order in which information will be fed into it (e.g., company name first, city, etc.).

NOTE: You will require a knowledge of DOS file structures to effectively import data. The firm whose database you are importing can provide the file layout information necessary to make this work properly.

5. User-defined fields to define prospect interest and demographic information.

   User-defined fields are used to capture important or industry-specific information on your OTDBs.

   Required Software Functions:

   - User-defined fields available in contact database. You need to determine how many additional fields of information you need to track.

     NOTE: User-defined fields can be character-based (e.g., 20 alpha/numeric keyboard entries), date fields (mo/day/year), logical (one character—yes or no), or dollar fields with decimals ($xxx.xx). User-defined fields can also have attributes that force required input (field must have an input if the cursor moves to it); be written to a history file any time they are updated; or can be hidden or protected so that nonauthorized users cannot change their value.

   - Availability of searching and reporting by any selected fields in contact database (e.g., both system and user defined).

- Report writer able to access user-defined fields to create custom reports.

6. Track lead source ROI

   Required to manage the effectiveness of your marketing and sales efforts.

   Required Software Functions:

   - Lead source field in contact database (can be user defined).

   - Pop-up windows, containing your lead source options to assist in data entry accuracy.

   - Reporting available, showing number of contacts per lead source.

   NOTE: If you want to track revenue by lead source, you need to have software that captures your sales amounts by client. Some systems allow you to enter orders and perform invoicing.

Effectively managing your sales pipeline will allow you to become proactive in your selling efforts. Once you are able to measure the progress of your OTDBs through your sales pipeline, you can determine the effort required to achieve your sales numbers. The numbers game will be discussed in the next chapter.

Chapter 4

THE NUMBERS GAME—HOW TO WIN AT IT!

The essence of sales is a numbers game. Your income will be directly related to the number of viable sales opportunities you come in contact with. Of course, many factors will influence your income (size of sale, repeat business opportunities, etc.), but the common denominator is someone to sell to.

Looking at selling from a numbers perspective can provide valuable insight into how to sell smarter. How many suspects do you need to contact to find one viable prospect? How many prospects do you need to be working (needs analysis, presentation, proposal, etc.) to close one deal? Determining the effort required to accomplish your personal sales objectives (or imposed quotas) is essential if you are going to be successful over the long haul.

The first step in winning at the numbers game is setting a target to aim for. If you have no target, or have nebulous goals, you have no means of tracking your performance or focusing your efforts. Setting goals in your sales career is similar to selecting a destination on a map (Figure 4–1). If you don't know where you are going, the chance that you will end up somewhere you want to be is totally dependent upon luck and the discretion of others. Managing your effort by the numbers gives you control over your destiny.

Determining your critical success factors and establishing the means to quantify them will provide you with the data you need to effectively manage the sales process and ensure positive results. Computers can be essential tools in managing the sales process only if you know *what* to manage. My experience indicates that usually there are no more than five critical success factors in any business process. You want to use the sales pipeline to define the activities that lead to the closing of business and determine which factors, if managed effectively, will lead to higher revenues, more profit, and happier clients. (All three items are typically interrelated.) The following are examples on how to measure critical success activities:

- Number of proposals presented within the last 30 days (or time frame it normally takes to close once the proposal is received)

- Number of prospect economic decision-makers contacted

- Number of suspects qualified into prospects

- Number of product demonstrations performed where the prospect requested additional information

- Number of referrals from customers, lead sources, and so on

- Number of face-to-face contacts with decision-makers

- Number of new accounts closed during the last 30 days

Figure 4–1   Selecting a Destination on a Map

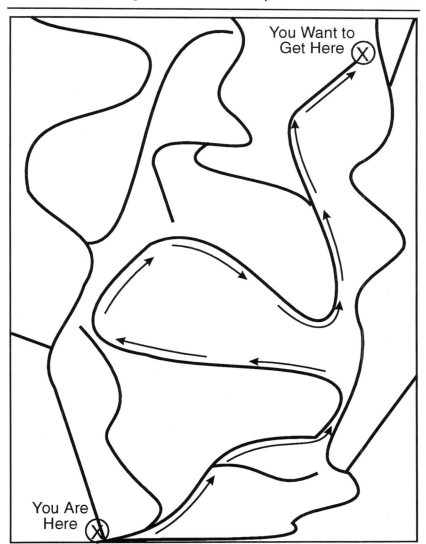

Selecting a destination (or goal) gives you the framework to
figure out how to get there from where you are!

How to Use Computers to Manage the Numbers Game

Contact management systems can allow salespeople and sales management to track and monitor their critical success factors and manage the sales pipeline with minimal effort. The basis of any selling situation comes down to the number of OTDBs you can get involved in. Improving your sales techniques or product/service quality may increase your selling ratios (number of opportunities divided by closed deals), but you still need to create enough contact opportunities to achieve your sales objectives.

Sales management systems can automatically track the activities being performed by a salesperson or sales team. Tracking the critical numbers (number of calls, meeting, proposals, etc.) can become a manual nightmare. Contact management software eliminates the need to manually track anything. A by-product of using the agenda and calendar functions of the software is a history file of all contacts with a particular account. (See the sample activity reports, summarized and detailed in Figures 4–2 and 4–3.)

The computer can track what was actually done. Comparing your targets against actual numbers guides you towards your sales goals.

Case Study: Managing by the Numbers

In the previous case study, we discussed the steps involved in managing your sales pipeline. The first few critical steps were to set targets and standards based on income goals and to determine the activities required to meet those goals. I will now elaborate on how to determine those numbers and provide further insights on how to use this valuable information.

One of my marketing plans involved selling packaged software solutions to mid-sized distributors, manufacturers, and other businesses needing financial management software. This presented several important factors that needed to be taken into consideration in order to develop a market plan or set targets to

Figure 4–2 Sample Activity Report—Summarized

ACTIVITY REPORT

Activity Period: 06/07/93 thru 06/11/93

AcctExec: JCL Jon C. Liberman

Date	Calls Count	Incoming Calls Count	Meetings Count	Letters Count	Orders Count	Tasks Count	Total Count
06/07/93	16	0	1	0	0	0	17
06/08/93	2	0	1	0	0	0	3
06/09/93	19	0	0	0	0	3	22
06/10/93	9	0	1	0	0	0	10
06/11/93	8	0	0	0	0	0	8
Total	54	0	3	0	0	3	60
Average	11	0	1	0	0	1	12

Figure 4-3   Sample Activity Report—Detail

DETAILED ACTIVITY REPORT

Activity Period: 06/07/93 thru 06/07/93

AcctExec: JCL Jon C. Liberman

Action	Date	Time	Length	Company	Contact	Objective	Results
Meeting	06/07/93	9:30A		Roscor Corp	Mitch Roston	Executive Survey	Deal Closed
Call	06/07/93	1:04P	0:01	Epko Industries	Al Rothchild	Sch project start	Left message
Call	06/07/93	1:08P	0:01	Finkle & Sons Company	Connie Derifield	F/U project	Left message
Call	06/07/93	1:08P	0:01	Health Plan Management, I	Scott Smiricky	Close Sale	Left message
Call	06/07/93	1:11P		The Chamberlain Group, In	James Gothard	Follow up on Account	Completed
Call	06/07/93	1:12P	0:01	BuchBinder	Carl Kuhns	F/U Project proposal	Left message
Call	06/07/93	1:13P	0:01	Alberto Culver Company	Norb Brand	f/u Powerhouse ap	Left message
Call	06/07/93	1:14P	0:01	Learning Resources	Lee Jennings	Varnet Demo	Left message
Call	06/07/93	1:19P		Schuessler Knitting Mills	Robert Schuessler	F/U Bob - Tim status	Completed
Call	06/07/93	1:25P	0:01	Great Lakes Graphics	Monique Daniel	Follow up on Account	Left message
Call	06/07/93	1:26P	0:01	Nichols - Homeshield	Brad Minkel	Close - Lou or Brad	Left message
Call	06/07/93	1:28P	0:01	Babson Brothers Co.	Maurice "Bud" Rich	Call Bud - sch mt/Bo	Left message
Call	06/07/93	1:32P	0:01	TSI	Wally Brabec	Follow up on Account	Left message
Call	06/07/93	2:14P	0:01	Health O Meter	Jay Rabinowitz	F/U Ray Cebold - AIC	Left message
Call	06/07/93	2:19P		Trucut	Steve Lebar	Sch fact find - <9am	cb 3 wks
Call	06/07/93	2:20P	0:01	H2O Plus, Inc.	Jim Magee	Follow up on Account	Left message
Call	06/07/93	2:26P		Cogan and McNabola	Mike Cogan	F/U LAN - Andy Cohen	No decision yet

manage my sales pipeline. (You will discover market planning and managing the sales pipeline are closely related.)

- The decision-making process tends to take six-plus months, and multiple people are involved in the process.

- Because of the cost of business computer systems and the tremendous disruption to a business that typically takes place, people tend to need a high level of confidence prior to buying anything. This requires a provider of business systems to build a strong relationship with the prospect before they will be comfortable purchasing anything.

- The effort involved (in time) to establish this kind of a relationship with a prospect is very high. As a result, we needed to qualify prospects effectively prior to investing all the required time.

- Given the fact that we needed to build a strong relationship with our clients prior to closing the deal, we discovered that demonstrating our software prematurely (before we had established a strong connection with the prospect) typically resulted in very poor closing ratios. We decided to postpone demonstrations until we understood in detail what the prospect was trying to accomplish, and we got them to invest time in us. This is an important item in determining which critical success factors to measure.

- The solutions we are selling cost anywhere from $35,000 to $300,000. Our prospects need to generate over $5 million in sales to afford such a product.

- We are looking for quality relationships with our clients, as opposed to volume sales. The labor required to successfully implement a sophisticated business computer system is quite involved. When we make a client happy, the opportunities for repeat business are high.

I am going into some detail here to provide you with an understanding of how the *process* of determining targets works. Every company that sells something to somebody will go through a similar process regardless of what they are selling.

Based upon the above factors, I established the following targets (and rationale):

- My goal was to sell four systems within 12 months. (Remember, this was only one of several product lines I was selling.)

- I closed roughly one deal out of two prospects at the Closing the Deal Stage. (Remember, we wouldn't present a detailed solution or demonstration until we got the prospect to invest time in us.)

- I presented roughly one proposal for every two prospects at the Developing a Solution Stage. (In some instances the prospect would decide to put off doing anything, or the prospect was not qualified, etc.)

- I gained commitment from one prospect to develop a solution out of every three prospects at the Prospect Stage.

- I found roughly one prospect from every five suspects fed into my sales pipeline. (Remember, we used targeted lists, referrals from vendors, etc. These were not Yellow Page suspects. If you use Yellow Pages or poorly defined sources, your ratios will be substantially lower.)

- Based upon the above assumptions, the targets in my sales pipeline for this one product line were as follows:

Targets: In order to close four deals within a 12-month period, I needed to generate 240 suspects (20 a month), from which 48 would become viable prospects and 16 would move into the Developing a Solution Stage (both my firm and the client invest time); I would present detailed proposals and demonstrate my solution to eight firms, of which four would buy.

These targets are very useful because they allow me to manage my efforts over the long haul, providing me the best opportunity to reach my income goals. I can evaluate on a monthly and quarterly basis how my sales pipeline looks for each product line. If my ratios change (for instance, seven suspects needed to generate one viable prospect), I can change my targets and adapt my effort accordingly. I know today where my commissions in three or four months are going to come from (given the six-month sales cycle).

The process of establishing targets and managing your sales pipeline to reach those targets will educate you about the critical success factors involved in whatever you happen to sell. Most successful salespeople understand the importance of these numbers instinctively. Sales and contact management systems can provide you with the means of easily managing this process.

By using the targets as described above, I have been able to consistently meet my financial objectives and manage my sales effort to continue doing so in the future.

Managing your sales efforts "by the numbers" puts you in the position to be "in the right place at the right time." The next chapter will elaborate on how you can use computers to manage this critical process to make more sales.

Summary

Before we list the software features and functions needed to utilize the concepts elaborated in Chapter 4, let's review what we have learned:

1. The essence of sales is a numbers game. Your income will be directly related to the number of viable sales opportunities you come in contact with. Of course, many factors will influence your income (size of sale, repeat business

opportunities, etc.), but the common denominator is someone to sell to.

2. The first step in winning at the numbers game is setting a target to aim for. If you have no target, or have nebulous goals, you have no means of tracking your performance or focusing your efforts.

3. The process of establishing targets and managing your sales pipeline to reach these targets will educate you about the critical success factors involved in whatever you happen to sell.

4. Managing your sales efforts "by the numbers" puts you in the position to be "in the right place at the right time."

Software Features Checklist

The following features are necessary to utilize the concepts detailed in this chapter.

1. Activity reporting available for each salesperson, which tracks actual contacts and is updated as a by-product of recording activities completed (calls made, meetings, tasks completed, etc.).

   To win at the numbers game, you must have accurate information.

   Required Software Functions:

   • Activity history updated automatically upon update of phone call, meeting, task, letter, or other activity. (You may want the software to automatically record the user, time, and date stamp in the history file as well as record the objective and result of the activity.)

   • Salesperson or account executive field in record.

   • Report by salesperson stating activity for period of time—both summary and detailed.

- Pop-up windows containing your sales pipeline steps to assist in data entry accuracy when inputting progress/sales cycle field.

- Report showing number of contacts per sales pipeline step (or progress level).

2. Market plan management (mailing lists and market segmentation).

   Market plan management or action plans allow you to set up multiple steps you may want to take on a select group of OTDBs. Mailing campaigns or filters can be used to target market to the selected group.

   Required Software Functions:

   - Means of sorting contact records by market plan (or mailing list) affiliation.

   - Ability to set up multiple steps in market plan to define activity to be accomplished (e.g., step one: send XYZ form letter; step two: call after seven days to follow up; step three: schedule meeting, etc.).

   - Report or inquiry of members in market plan.

   - **OPTIONAL:** Some market plan systems can create agenda items (calls, letters, tasks) for salespeople automatically. When you run the automatic agenda activity creation function, it creates the agenda items for each salesperson and will come up on their to-do lists.

   - Report showing number of contacts per sales pipeline step, by market plan.

3. Bulk Mailings use various selection criteria to send a form letter to a group of OTDBs. Examples of selection criteria could include all retail businesses over $5 million in sales in a particular zip code. Bulk mailing provides tremendous productivity tools for any sales organization

because of the number of personalized contacts that can be made with minimal clerical labor.

Required Software Functions:

- Ability to sort OTDBs into groups or mailing lists. Marketing plan systems provide this capability, as do other selection-based systems.

- Ability to select a group in the Contact Management system and merge the contact name, company name, address, city, state, zip code, and salutation with a form letter in a word processor.

- Automatic update of the history file with the form letter name and date.

4. Budget versus actual reporting provides management with a tool to manage the sales pipeline, quota, and budgetary processes. Comparing a budget to actual numbers gives you the means of measuring how well you are doing against your objectives (targets).

Required Software Functions:

- Fields in the contact management system that allow the input of target or budget numbers.

- Activity reporting that tracks actual numbers based on the information you wish to compare to budget.

- In some instances, a report writer will be required along with user-defined fields to capture the necessary information.

Chapter 5

BEING IN THE RIGHT PLACE AT THE RIGHT TIME

This chapter discusses using a computerized follow-up system to be in the right place at the right time. The "right place" is in front of (in contact with) the prospective buyer. The "right time" is when your OTDB (prospect) is ready to buy a product or service you can sell.

Selling is really not very complicated. You simply need to be in front of the prospect when they have the need for your product/service and to make them feel comfortable that the benefits they will receive by hiring you will outweigh the risks.

The trick is knowing *when* to be in front of the OTDB and how to position yourself in their mind so they feel safe with you. What makes this a challenge is that people and businesses tend not to plan, but to react. You can discuss the needs of a business with upper management, and they might tell you all about their "plans" for expansion, upgrading their systems, and so on. But they tend to act only when something in their environment forces them to.

An effective, computerized sales management system will provide you with the tool to keep in front of your OTDBs on a regular basis. The goal is to be in contact with enough of the right people (OTDBs), at the right firms, on a consistent basis over time.

How to Use Computers to Be at the Right Place at the Right Time

Sales management systems can provide daily call lists, agendas, and to-do lists to ensure that opportunities are not missed. The following five-step process will enable you to be at the right place at the right time.

Step 1

Automate your sales force with software that provides automated "tickler lists" and agenda management functions.

Tickler lists are daily lists of OTDBs that need something done (a phone call, letter, proposal, etc.). You need the system to allow you to prioritize your to-do list. The goal is to simplify the process of ensuring nothing is forgotten or left out. It is very helpful when the software provides a simple inquiry screen that lists, by priority and date/time scheduled, all the activities you have scheduled for the day, so you can review them with a quick glance. Most systems will print out this information in report format, but I have found it very useful to see it all on the screen at one time.

Agenda management functions enable you to schedule events and review a calendar easily. Pop-up windows that display daily, weekly, and monthly schedules facilitate scheduling while you're on the phone with your OTDB. Some software checks for schedule conflicts. When you schedule an event (phone call, meeting, etc.), you input the amount of time the item will take; if you have two events scheduled with overlapping time frames, the system will inform you of the conflict.

The purpose of the computer system is to simplify the process of following up phone calls and tasks. The goal is to not drop any balls or miss any opportunities. To accomplish these goals, the software must provide the following functions:

- You need the software to easily allow for the scheduling of activities. Pop-up calendars that input selected date fields into the next action field are very useful. (See Figure 5–1.)

Figure 5–1 Sample Pop-Up Calendar Window in Activity Scheduling Screen

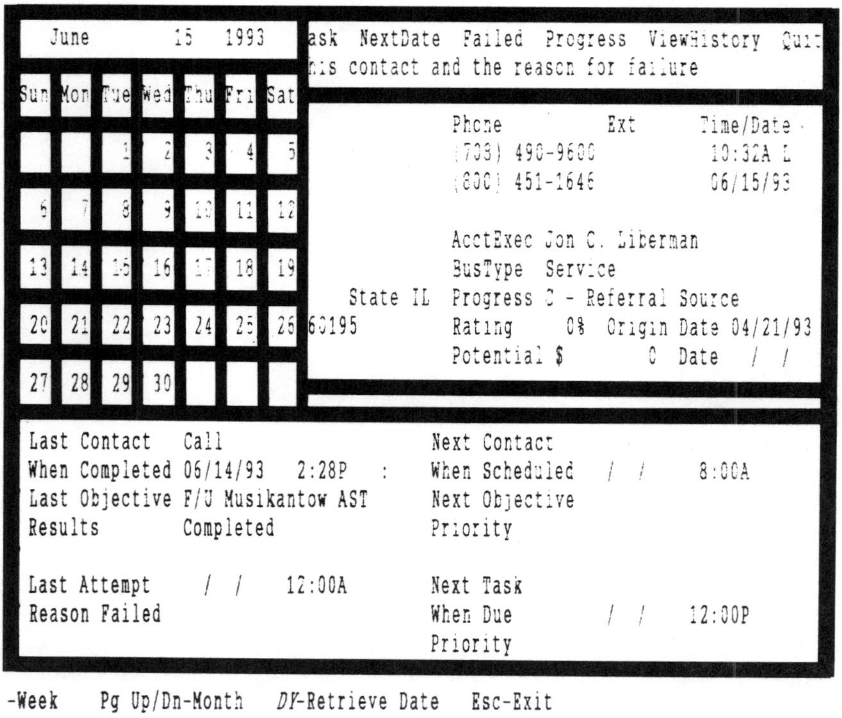

- The system needs to provide on-line inquiry of to-do lists, sorted by priority and due date (Figure 5–2). Some people can utilize reports that show the activities scheduled to do, although on-line inquiry simplifies immediate review.

- The software needs to provide free-form notes to remind the salesperson of previous conversations, commitments, and important information (Figure 5–3).

Step 2

Have a clear picture of what your best prospects look like. What are their demographics? Who is the contact person? How do they

Figure 5–2   Sample Daily To-Do List—On-Line

Calls

Company	Objective/Task	Date	Time	Priority
Finkle & Sons Company	F/U project	06/15/93	8:00A	Critical
EBT-Division of In Step E	Close Sale	06/15/93	8:00A	Critical
Sysnet Computer Systems,	Sch demo for 7/8 1030a	06/15/93	8:00A	Critical
Peters Machinery Co.	Follow up on Account	06/15/93	8:00A	Critical
Chicago Social Club	Introduce CS&R - Overv	06/15/93	8:00A	Critical
Nichols - Homeshield	Sch kick off mt	06/15/93	8:00A	Critical
John Sexton Contractors C	Follow up on Account	06/15/93	8:00A	Critical
EXIMIOUS	Get info from Jerry	06/15/93	8:00A	Critical
CS&R Henry Cairo	Call Owen & Al - lease	06/15/93	8:00A	Critical
Health Plan Management, I	Close Sale	06/15/93	8:00A	Critical
J.C. Schultz Enterprises,	F/U Sel Service	06/15/93	8:00A	Critical
Reed-Chatwood, Inc.	Follow up on letter	06/15/93	8:00A	Critical
Parsons Deleuw	F/U Univell Lead	06/15/93	8:00A	Critical
Alberto Culver Company	f/u Powerhouse ap	06/15/93	8:00A	Critical
LaSalle Partners	F/U Rich Lee - new bos	06/15/93	8:00A	Critical
Astor Development	Follow up on Account	06/15/93	8:00A	Critical
Progress Software	follow up for referral	06/15/93	8:00A	Critical

DY-Select Backspace-Clear

Figure 5–3   Sample Notes Field

```
CONTACT
Goto  Track  Agenda  Edit  Dial  Plan  Letter  Order  View  Script  Report  Quit
Display and select contacts scheduled to be worked with
```

```
Company Interactive                    Phone          Ext      Time/Date
Contact John Overend                   (708) 490-9600          10:35A L
Title   VP                             (830) 451-1646          06/15/93
Dear:   John
Address 2401 Hassell rd                AcctExec Jon C. Liberman
        Suite 1500                     BusType  Service
City    Hoffman Estates      State IL  Progress C - Referral Source
Country USA           Zip 60195        Rating    0%  Origin Date 04/21/93
Source  Personal/JCL                   Potential $       0  Date   /  /
```

```
NOTES
06/14/93 - John AST problem  was with setup ROM; Name of referral -
06/03/93 - Tim Scheele has lead for me; Been burned on Unix programming -
05/20/93 - Hillary, 5% of dealer value = 1st yr warranty; additional 5% for
Ontario -
04/28/93 - John, (I need Sifa quote); will fax me quote asap. He'll call me
tommorrow
```

```
Record 526     of 541    Index Company   Filter OFF               Call OFF
```

make decisions? What problems are they experiencing? In other words, develop an Ideal Customer Profile. (See Figure 5–4. How to develop an Ideal Customer Profile is described in detail in the Case Study later in this chapter.)

The Ideal Customer Profile acts as a filter to screen suspects and determine if they should be pursued, and if so on what basis. When contacting a prospect, ask questions that help you determine where the prospect fits your ideal candidate, and where they do not.

Figure 5–4   Ideal Customer Profile

Gives you the filter that enables you to aim your selling efforts.

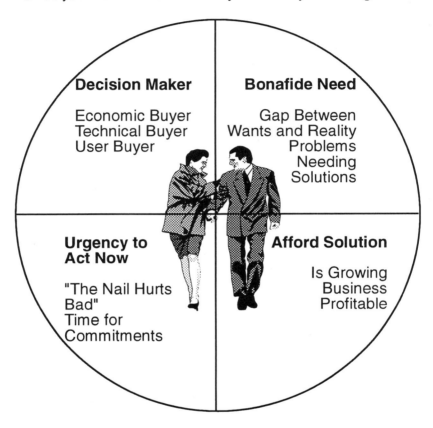

Use questions to determine potentials. Compare to your Ideal Customer Profile.

What you are attempting to accomplish in the questioning process is an understanding of the potential of the prospect. If you believe the prospect will buy your product/service from somebody in the future, put the prospect in your follow-up system. Telemarketing scripts can assist in ensuring the appropriate questions are being asked on a consistent basis.

Step 3

Based upon their responses, determine how often you should keep in front on them. "Keeping in front" can take many forms. You can phone them or meet them at the office, invite them to a function (a sports event, for example), or mail something to them, (direct mail, newsletter, etc.), although face-to-face visits or phone calls tend to be more effective, especially with hot prospects.

As prospects progress through your sales pipeline, you should keep in contact with them more regularly. As a rule of thumb, the follow-up programs illustrated in Figure 5–5 may be helpful.

Step 4

Work your follow-up system. The advantages of computerized follow-up systems are obvious once you use one. But the process described will work with manual or card systems also, if used properly. Each time you contact the prospect, you want to revisit the commitments or plans they described in earlier contacts. You also want to ask questions that will uncover new opportunities. Remember, most people tend to react rather than plan. The goal is to contact them when their need for your firm is strong.

Surveys have revealed that the typical sale takes over five contacts from initial cold call to closed deal. The surveys also have shown that the typical salesperson quits after the first call (and rejection). The lesson is that multiple contacts over time are required to generate sales. The Ideal Customer Profile can improve your batting average by helping you focus your efforts on OTDBs

Figure 5-5   Sales Pipeline Management: Keeping in Front of the OTDB

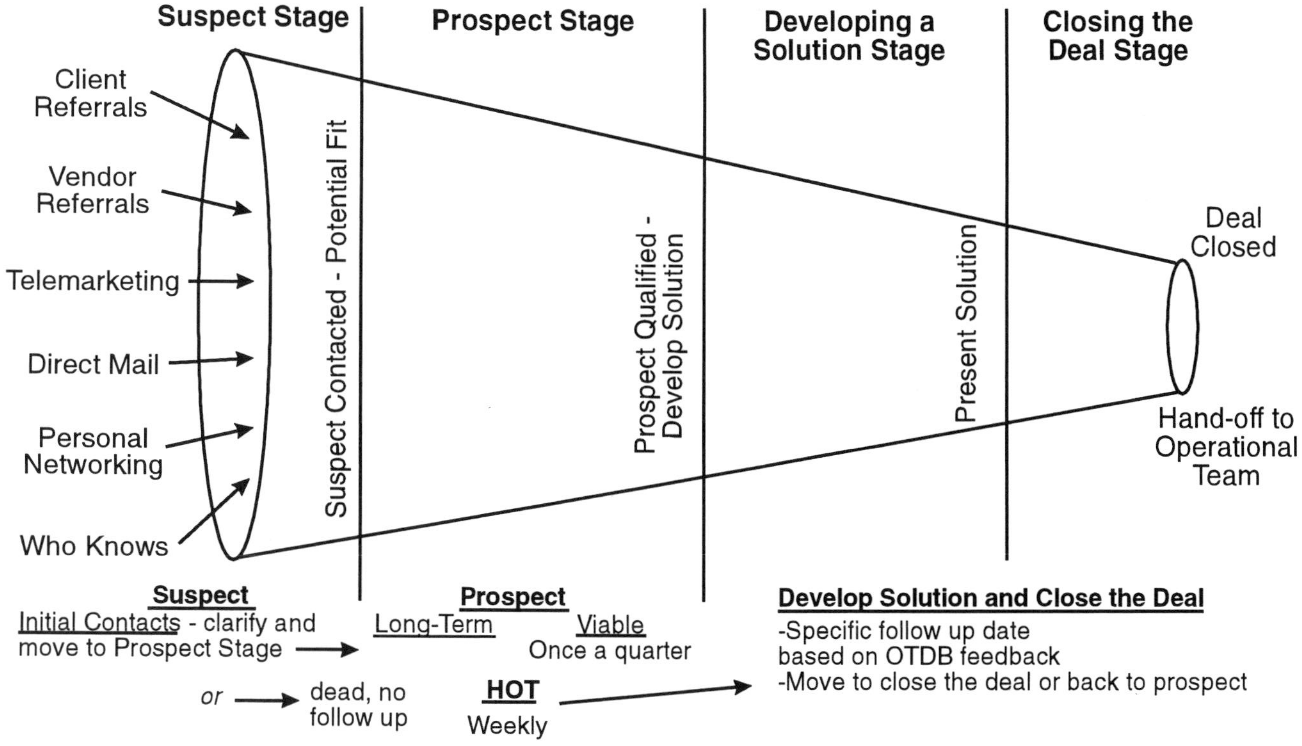

Suspect Stage | Prospect Stage | Developing a Solution Stage | Closing the Deal Stage

Client Referrals
Vendor Referrals
Telemarketing
Direct Mail
Personal Networking
Who Knows

Suspect Contacted - Potential Fit
Prospect Qualified - Develop Solution
Present Solution
Deal Closed
Hand-off to Operational Team

Suspect
Initial Contacts - clarify and move to Prospect Stage

or → dead, no follow up

Prospect
Long-Term — Viable
Once a quarter

HOT
Weekly

Develop Solution and Close the Deal
-Specific follow up date based on OTDB feedback
-Move to close the deal or back to prospect

with the best odds of buying your product/service. *But consistent follow-up is required to be at the right place at the right time!*

Step 5

Continue to work your follow-up system. Multiple contacts over time build a relationship with the prospect. After four or five conversations, you are no longer a total stranger. If you have a real intention of helping the OTDB resolve their problems—by sending appropriate articles and information, for example—you will build the foundation for a relationship. When the account finally needs your product/service, in the short term you have an advantage. If you satisfy their needs, you have the basis for an ongoing, win-win relationship.

The focal point of this follow-up approach involves using the computer as a tool to simplify the process of keeping in contact with multiple OTDBs over time.

Benefits of Automated Follow-Up Systems

There are many advantages to this follow-up system:

- People don't plan; they react to immediate needs. A managed follow-up system will give you a higher chance of being in front of the prospect when their need for a solution is ripe.

- Multiple contacts over time give the prospect the feeling that you will be around for the long haul. This provides them the perspective that you can be trusted and will be there when they need you.

- By working this system, you will learn how to improve your qualifying process. As you track your results over time, you will begin to improve your ability to spot opportunities where you never would have seen them in the past and to learn which ones not to bother with. One common mistake of salespeople is to focus their attention only on the accounts that seem to be buying in the near future. I'm not suggesting these hot prospects aren't viable; I'm suggesting that a lot of excellent sales opportunities are passed up because their immediate needs haven't blossomed.

- Automated contact management systems will enable you to keep in contact with a large number of prospects and customers with minimal effort and without dropping any balls. By working your prospect database in this manner, you can focus the attention where it's required, on the hot deals, while not allowing other future possibilities to pass you by.

- You can use the demographic and industry-specific information you gather to target specific accounts that fit profiles for hot prospects. For instance, if a new development in your industry occurs (such as competition going out of business or a new product), you can quickly and easily locate prospects who would benefit from this change. Direct-mail campaigns or telemarketing efforts based upon these opportunities can reap great rewards.

- You can use the custom notes features of contact management software to personalize your message. Relating to specific things the prospect said in a previous conversation gives them the impression you are a professional who cares about them. Making the person on the other end of the phone believe that you remember the details produces a feeling of confidence and trust, both essential if you are going to convince them to give you money (close the deal). Examples of personalized notes include specific dates mentioned for meeting to decide something; competitors they are talking to; products they presently use; or any details that would be useful to you when talking with this OTDB in the future.

Being in the right place at the right time also makes sense with customer service.

How to Use Computers to Keep Your Clients

As I've previously mentioned, keeping your hard-won clients happy can provide excellent returns on your investment in time. Microcomputers can provide the tools for a salesperson to apply the same principles of follow-up and time management to customer service.

Regardless of whether you sell a product or service, keeping in touch with your clients—especially after work is performed, a problem is resolved, or a delivery is made—is good customer service. Even if there is a problem with your product/service, the fact that you called to make sure they're happy makes your clients feel you care and are looking out for their best interests.

Contact management software can also assist you in communicating with people in your organization whom you rely on to service your clients. *Timely follow-up and living up to commitments are essential for long-term customer satisfaction.* Use the "tickler" follow-up capabilities of contact management software to schedule customer service calls and tasks.

Another benefit of making these customer service follow-up calls is the opportunity to sell additional products/services. I typically ask a client, after ensuring they're satisfied with what they've just experienced (service provided, product used, etc.) if there is any other area in which we can be of service. You can probe with questions to uncover future opportunities. Asking for referrals at this time will also provide excellent results.

Excellent communication between your sales force, service staff, and production people (whoever produces whatever it is you sell) is essential to maintain high levels of customer service.

Computer systems using electronic mail programs can eliminate missed messages and ensure timely communication.

Using Contact Management Software to Ensure Excellent Customer Service

I have never seen a business that didn't, at least occasionally, have a customer service problem. Product defects, shipping difficulties, service timeliness—Murphy's famous law surely exists in today's business world.

Customer attitudes are shaped more by how your organization handles (or avoids) problems than by any other act. A simple phone call following up on your client to ensure they're happy gives you a proactive means of managing your customer service. When a customer calls you, requesting information or complaining about something, use your tickler system to schedule the appropriate follow-up. If someone in your firm needs to do something to resolve the problem, put a tickler in your system to ensure they do their job. You actually can save yourself a great deal of time (and lost clients) by being the conscience for your support staff.

I put all my follow-up activities—prospect calls, customer service calls, tasks to do—in one tickler system. That way, I have only one place to look to ensure I don't forget anything. I prioritize each activity and make sure I complete the critical priorities every day. (See Figure 5–6.)

Once again, the discipline of effective time management is critical. As soon as the customer issue comes to your attention, determine the appropriate course of action and input the follow-up steps in your system. When one of my associates gives me a commitment as to when they will do something for my client, especially if it's an important task, I record my follow-up in my system. You'd be amazed at how efficient someone will be when they know someone's going to follow up.

Figure 5–6   Sample Call List, Prioritized

Calls

Company	Objective/Task	Date	Time	Priority
Continental Glass & Plast	Follow up on Account	06/21/93	8:00A	Critical
Spinak, Levinson & Babcoc	Collect $	06/21/93	8:00A	Critical
Catholic Charities	Follow up on Account	06/21/93	8:00A	Critical
Reynolds Machine & Tool C	Follow up on Account	06/21/93	8:00A	Critical
Metraflex	F/U Progress-Varnet	06/21/93	8:00A	Critical
Dayton Osland & Assoc	F/U Bill	06/21/93	8:00A	Critical
River Forest Insurance Co	Close Sale	06/21/93	8:00A	Critical
Brush Fuses, Inc.	Follow up on Account	06/21/93	8:00A	Critical
Service Web Offset Corp	F/U Selection Serv	06/21/93	8:00A	Critical
Tassani Communications	Follow up on Account	06/21/93	8:00A	Critical
Tomahawk II, Inc.	Follow up on Account	06/21/93	8:00A	Critical
Heller & Richmond, Ltd	F/U ltr	06/21/93	8:00A	Critical
Emergency Physicians Grou	Follow up on Account	06/21/93	8:00A	Critical
Romano Brothers Beverage	F/U LAN & Progress	06/21/93	8:00A	Critical
Hearn Company	Follow up on Account	06/21/93	8:00A	Critical
Draw Enterprises, Inc.	Follow up on Account	06/21/93	8:00A	High
AMCO Corporation	F/U Joyce	06/21/93	8:00A	High

D↑-Select Backspace-Clear

Developing and Using an Ideal Customer Profile

The Ideal Customer Profile is a useful tool to quickly evaluate suspects and prospects to determine how to best act towards the account in order to maximize your ROI. In other words, if you minimize the time you waste contacting unqualified leads and following up with businesses that you probably won't sell, or if you do sell, that probably won't be happy, you maximize the time you can spend on viable prospects (OTDBs).

Ideal Customer Profiles can be developed for specific product lines or to define the characteristics of the type of client you want to establish a relationship with, regardless of the products/services you can sell. In the following example, I will classify the characteristics of the type of client relationship I am looking to establish. The various products and services I sell can modify this profile, but the basics still apply.

Sample Ideal Client Profile

My Ideal Client has these characteristics:

1. **A profitable business in a growth mode—gross sales ranging from 20 to 250 million with increases of 10–20 percent per year.**

   Expanding businesses are more prone to change their status quo to keep up with their growth. Their need for change provides me an opportunity to sell something.

2. **Allows me access to their key decision-makers. I need to talk to the people who sign the checks (or okay disbursements).**

   I sell services and products that typically cost a lot of money and have major effects on an organization. As a result, these decisions will only be made after the people who control the money are comfortable with the risk. I want to establish a positive relationship with these people.

3. **Clear objectives and a willingness to commit resources to achieve those objectives.**

   If the client is uncertain about what they want to accomplish, or no clear consensus exists among management, they will not spend money. If the client is unwilling to commit the resources required to do the job right, I don't want to get involved with them.

4. **Minimal internal data processing or information management resources.**

   One of our major competitive advantages is our people and the services we can provide to help our clients use technology more effectively. If the client has large internal staffs who perform (theoretically) these same services, we are viewed as competition. In these situations the sale usually comes down to one of price (versus value), and the opportunity for us to bill for services is diminished.

5. **Needs what we can sell them. We can provide value (service/product) that helps our client meet or exceed their objectives.**

   If we can not help the client improve their situation, I do not want to waste my time. I'm looking for long-term relationships.

6. **Desire for a "win-win" relationship.**

   Some people feel they only win if you lose (in terms of negotiating, taking advantage, etc.). These types I wish on my competition.

7. **An on-going business relationship is available that generates opportunities to do business in the future.**

   The cost of closing the initial deal with a client is quite substantial. Repeat business from happy clients allows me to leverage my efforts and maximize my earnings.

How to Use This Profile to Qualify Prospects

When you are qualifying a prospect, ask them questions that will reveal how the person (and firm) fits your Ideal Profile. For instance, are you talking to the person who will sign the check (or has authority to okay the purchase)? Is the firm committed to doing something? What services or products do they think they need? Can they afford the solution they will need? What kind of internal resources do they have?

Their responses will determine how well they fit your ideal. Closely follow up those that come close to fitting the ideal characteristics. Make a judgement call on those that only partially fit the profile. *I am not suggesting you only call on ideal candidates, only that you focus your priority time on those that are the closest fit.*

You can get differing impressions of a business from talking to different people in the firm. You need to dig to understand what the real characteristics are and to determine if an investment in time is worthwhile.

How to Use the Ideal Profile to Target Suspects to Contact

The profile can be very useful in determining who to feed into your sales pipeline. In my case, I was able to locate lists of businesses in my geographic market who are growing by over 15 percent per year, or who are in growth industries. I also read newspapers and business journals, targeting my geographic area to locate businesses to feed into my sales pipeline.

Brainstorming sessions with other sales/marketing people in your firm using the Ideal Customer Profile as food for thought can often provide excellent ideas for locating sources of leads.

Using the Ideal Customer Profile is a creative exercise. It's more like an art form than a science. But it can be very useful in finding and screening OTDBs and determining the best course of action to take with them.

How to Use the Ideal Customer Profile with Your Sales Management System

Sales management systems can assist you in utilizing the concept of the Ideal Customer Profile in two major ways:

1. Computerized sales scripts can help telemarketers and salespeople follow effective questioning procedures. You can use the experience of your more effective salespeople to develop the best questions and responses to

objections. Many sales systems allow for multiple branches in their scripts, whereby, dependent upon the prospect's response, you can provide suggestions to the salesperson as to what to say. This allows you to provide salespersons with suggestions about how to answer a variety of prospect responses. (See Figure 5–7.)

My experience has suggested that most effective sales-people make their sales pitch their own and won't follow, word for word, a sales script. On the other hand, while selling on the phone, scripts that outline good ideas and

Figure 5–7   Sample Script with Branch Menu

```
TEST SCRIPT
Yes No Continue Previous Script Quit
Branch to 'NEXT' paragraph in script
```

```
Script SA-MPE   Description Sample Script

Yes  -     No  -     Continue  -
```

```
Have you heard of the U.S.A. ?
```

suggestions can be very helpful in overcoming objections and assisting in covering all the bases.

2. User-defined fields can track unique or pertinent information that can enhance the Ideal Customer Profile techniques to make more sales. Every business product and service is purchased by the customer to solve a particular problem and provide specific benefits. Sales management software that allows you to track specific information that assists your selling situation can provide invaluable information to target your selling efforts. The challenge is to define in consistent and exact terms specific sales criteria and to locate (search your database for) OTDBs that match your criteria.

For instance, if you sell a product or service that is based on the use of technology (computer systems, medical equipment, manufacturing machinery, etc.), the ability to track what type of technology your OTDB presently is using and how long they have been using it could be very valuable. When a new development in the marketplace makes a particular product obsolete (for instance, a competitor goes out of business or a new technology emerges), the ability to quickly locate all the OTDBs in your database that use that competitor's product and, for example, mail them something or target them for calling, can reap great rewards.

In this case, you would need a field in your database into which you could input who your competitor is and what technology they are using. Pop-up windows that allow you to predefine entries ensure consistent data input and data accuracy.

Every industry has it's own unique nomenclature and terminology. The use of User-defined fields allows each sales team to develop their own useful database of information and helps determine where the best sales opportunities exist. The following are examples of User-defined fields you may need in your system:

- Areas of interest (products, services, problems, etc.)
- Competitors
- Technologies/products being used
- Sales volume, number of employees
- Subsidiaries or parent company
- Number of locations
- Decision-makers—additional contacts
- Stated business objectives
- Number of internal support staff
- Targeted products/services to sell
- Decision time frame
- Lead source
- Business type or SIC (Standard Industrial Classification) code
- Maintenance or other renewal dates
- CPA, lawyer, and/or other professional advisors
- Personal information on key contact (birthday, number of children, etc).

Case Study—An Example of Being in the Right Place at the Right Time

Earlier I described my Ideal Client Profile. I closed one of my largest clients because I used this Ideal Customer Profile process to uncover a goldmine. I discovered this client by accident. I had received 12 references from a software firm we represent. This client was one of those references. When I called the Director of Information Services at this reference, we discussed how he felt about the software his organization had been using for the previous two years. Typically, I try to use every contact with an OTDB to uncover opportunities. I asked the director questions to help me evaluate how they compared to my Ideal Client Profile. I discovered that they fit the profile very well:

- They are a $30 million organization that has recently experienced rapid expansion.

- I had access to one of the key decision-makers. (The Director of I.S. was responsible for spending his budget.)

- The client expressed definite and clear objectives for major applications that had been committed to implementation. (One problem was that they had hired a competitor to design the new systems prior to my phone call.)

- Although the client had some internal data processing staff, they had no one with the time to take on new projects and were not expecting to hire additional staff.

- The client had no immediate need for our products or services but suggested I keep in contact with him because he might in the future.

- It was difficult for me to determine whether the Director of I.S. valued "win-win" relationship with the vendors and suppliers they purchase from. At least I didn't have a negative impression.

- They seemed to be an excellent prospect judging by the nature and size of the future projects we spoke about.

At the end of my discussion with the Director of I.S., I asked if he would mind if I kept in contact with him because I felt we could be of service at some point in the future. He said he didn't mind.

I contacted this OTDB, via phone calls and letters, twelve times during the next 18 months. I talked with managers who reported to the Director of I.S., sent them promo literature and articles, asked how their projects were going, and so on. After the twelfth contact I was finally able to schedule a meeting to discuss a new problem. To make a long story short, since that meeting we have billed over $90,000 in professional fees and have targeted several new projects that will generate over $100,000 more in billing over the next year.

I knew that if I kept in front of this account, an opportunity would eventually arise. I wanted to make sure I was in the right place at the right time.

Keeping in contact with hundreds of OTDBs takes a considerable amount of time. In the next chapter we will discuss the secrets of making time work for you.

Summary

Before we list the software features and functions needed to utilize the concepts elaborated in Chapter 5, let's review what we have learned.

1. Selling is really not very complicated. You simply need to be in front of the prospect when they have the need for your product/service and to make them feel comfortable that the benefits they will receive by hiring you will outweigh the risks.

2. An effective sales management system will enable you to keep in front of your prospects and customers on a regular basis. The key is to be in contact with enough of the right people (OTDBs), at the right firms, on a consistent basis over time.

3. The Ideal Customer Profile is a useful tool to quickly evaluate suspects and prospects to determine how to best act towards the account in order to maximize your return

on investment. In other words, if you minimize the time you waste contacting unqualified leads and following up with businesses that you probably won't sell—or, if you do sell, that you probably can't satisfy—you maximize the time you can spend on viable prospects (OTDBs).

4. The focal point of this follow-up approach involves using the computer to simplify the process of keeping in contact with multiple OTDBs over time. The objectives of your initial contacts are to effectively qualify the prospect to determine how well they fit your Ideal Customer Profile and to determine how often, and using what means, to keep in contact with them.

5. Timely follow-up and living up to commitments are essential for long-term customer satisfaction. Use the tickler follow-up capabilities of contact management software to schedule customer service calls and tasks.

6. Customer attitudes are shaped more by how your organization handles (or avoids) problems than by any other act. A simple phone call following up on your clients to ensure they're happy gives you a proactive means of managing your customer service.

Software Features Checklist

To successfully utilize a contact management system to be at the right place at the right time, the following features are necessary.

1. Automated "tickler" system.

    The software must remind you of all the activities you want to accomplish, sorted by date and priority. The system should allow you to review all scheduled activities by date and to select the one you want to act upon, thereby bringing up that record.

Required Software Functions:

- Field(s) for scheduling activities in account record. Some software allows you to schedule only one or two items at a time for a particular record. Others enable you to schedule unlimited activities per record.

- Ability to see on-line daily to-do lists easily and to pull up selected accounts for action (call, task, etc.).

- Pop-up calendar to input date into field for scheduling activities that allow week- and month-at-a-glance inquiry.

- **Optional:** Audio or visual alarms that notify you of a scheduled activity.

- Date conflict alarm that notifies you when an activity conflicts with a previously scheduled activity.

2. Integrated word processor (w/p) for personalized or form letters.

   Sending personalized letters or doing bulk mailings requires a word processor be integrated with your contact management system. Two main options exist:

   i. Contact management software's own integrated w/p module. Typically these w/p packages are not as full-featured as popular stand-alone w/p packages (such as WordPerfect, Microsoft Word, Word Star, etc.). If your needs are simple—one-page letters with minimal fancy features (highlighting, different fonts, italic, etc.)—these packages are fine.

   ii. Stand-alone word processing packages. These packages are usually much more powerful and full featured. You may already be using a stand-alone package in your office. In that case, you need the contact management software to seamlessly integrate with the w/p of your choice so that you do not need to duplicate your efforts.

Required Software Functions:

- Either Integrated w/p system or seamless tie-in to stand-alone package (e.g., name, address, salutation).

- Seamless integration enables you to not leave the CMS software system in order to select an OTDB to send either a personalized or form letter to.

NOTE: My intention here is simply to outline the software functions needed in the contact management software as it relates to word processing—not to describe all word processing functions *per se*.

- Ability to sort your OTDBs by user-defined fields so that you can select groups to send a form letter to.

3. Easy-to-use agenda management system.

The software should make it easy to schedule items, forward uncompleted tasks, and schedule activities.

Required Software Functions:

- The ability to schedule multiple activities per OTDB, to schedule each date with a pop-up calendar, to record the objective of each call, and to set a priority for each activity scheduled.

- The ability to forward all uncompleted items from one date to another.

- **OPTIONAL:** The ability to schedule recurring activities with one input (e.g., call this client once a month for the next three months).

- The ability to print out agendas and to-do lists by salesperson for any selected period of time.

Chapter 6

THE SECRETS OF MAKING TIME WORK FOR YOU

In modern society time is the scarcest resource. As salespeople, how we spend our time is probably the single most important decision we make that will directly affect our income. Yet time management is one of the most neglected aspects of sales management or selling in general. A computer system can help you spend your time more wisely—if you have the personal discipline required to use it wisely.

Have you ever evaluated, objectively, how you spend your time? How much do you actually spend selling as opposed to administering, doing paperwork, taking coffee breaks, and so on?

The only time you can make a sale is when you are in contact with an OTDB. Typically, there are only specific times during the day and week when you have the opportunity to contact an OTDB. It makes common sense to plan your investment in time to maximize these contacts. As simple as this may sound, the temptations and distractions that eat up your potential contact time are powerful and abundant.

The Black Hole/Loose Ends Syndrome

The concept of the black hole, that infinite place in space that consumes all light and energy, exists on most of our desks. We are all bombarded by information—commercials, junk mail, phone calls, constant interruptions—that saps our attention, unfocuses our efforts, and overwhelms most of us. One symptom of this exists in most of the in boxes on our desks! Paper piles up— things we need to do, read, evaluate, respond to. One way to measure how overwhelmed you are is to take out a ruler and measure how many inches of stuff is in your in box (or under your desk). How much of that stuff have you touched more than once? (See Figure 6–1.)

A wise man once revealed to me The Secret of Efficiency:

Do What You Do, When You Are Doing It!

In other words, finish one activity before starting another. In some situations, you can't totally finish an activity before something or someone interrupts, but you can ensure that you are not leaving any loose ends that will come back to haunt you later. Let's say you are writing a proposal, and you are not finished but you have an important appointment. Finish the paragraph (or thought) you are in the middle of and put the paper away in your file. Schedule time in your agenda when you will go back and finish the project before going to the next appointment.

Or when opening mail, determine what to do with the mail when you first touch it. Either put it in your filing system for future retrieval, send it to the appropriate individual, or trash it. Most mail, if not immediately useful, should be trashed, or it just piles up and you need to handle it a second, third, or fourth time.

When using a contact management software system, it is essential you follow this practice. If a good part of your day is

Figure 6–1   What Happens When Loose Ends Are Not Tied Up

spent selling on the phone, it is essential you have a software system that allows you to easily and quickly update your contact information *while you are on the phone*. When you hang up the phone, you need to have completed your data input.

One major downfall of not following this "touch it once" practice is that your information in the computer will never be up-to-date, and, if you are like most people, you will creatively avoid going back and inputting your information and notes. This often results in the system not being used and the benefits of automation being lost.

In my opinion, "loose ends" are the single greatest cause of crises management, stress, overwhelming workloads, and lost profits!

Sales/contact management software can help you manage time by automating your agenda, calendar, and activity lists.

Using Contact Management Software to Tie Up Loose Ends

Automated appointment, call, and task management systems can be invaluable in improving your productivity and minimizing loose ends. Automated appointment/call systems eliminate the need to rely on your memory or scraps of paper to keep track of all the things you need to do during your workday.

The danger of trying to rely on your memory, if you are like most people, is that it's too easy to forget. We are bombarded by so much information during the day and need to keep track of so many details that, without an organized system, we simply leave too many loose ends.

The following are recommendations on how to use a micro-computer with contact management software to manage your time:

1. Use the agenda and calendar functions of the software to schedule all your meetings, calls, and tasks. Having one place to look minimizes the opportunity to misplace or forget an important event or task. To be safe, I suggest

you also keep your appointments in a paper format (calendar, day-timer, etc.).

2. Each morning, refer to your calls and tasks lists, sorted by priority. Plan out when you will accomplish the critical priorities during the day. I refer to these lists throughout the day to ensure that I don't forget anything.

3. Update your agenda (meetings, calls, and tasks) immediately upon determining that something needs to be done. For example, when I complete a phone call to a prospect (or client, etc.), I determine when I should next follow this account up and immediately input the event into my agenda. If I need to write a letter or get some information, I update my system before I do anything else. This eliminates the potential of forgetting or having to go back and update the system later.

4. If I think of something important to do, and I'm not near my system, I make a note in my pocket calendar. As soon as I'm able, I enter the task into my agenda. This ensures I don't forget important tasks or waste time looking in shirt pockets for scraps of paper.

Case Study: An Example of Loose Ends Causing Inefficiencies

I know a salesman who provides a constant reminder to me of how loose ends cause crises and inefficiencies. This gentleman works harder than almost any other person I know. He is at work by 6:30 or 7:00 A.M. every day, and works until evening, six or seven days a week. He rarely takes a lunch, and his wife has to drag him on vacations. 70- to 80-hour work weeks are normal for him. In addition to working hard, this fellow is a genuinely nice guy; most people like him. Yet, despite his tremendous effort and personable disposition, he is only a little above average in terms of his sales and commissions.

He believes that he is very efficient—he maintains to-do lists of all the tasks he needs to complete each day (that turns into weeks and months), and even uses a sales management software system. The problem is that he is constantly attempting to do too much and chronically leaves loose ends. Here are some examples of loose ends he suffers from:

- He is rarely on time for meetings.

- He is continually working on proposals in a rush mode because they are due the next day.

- He rarely completes tasks on time; you need to remind him several times to get him to live up to his commitments.

- He never turns in critical paperwork on time, even when not doing so affects his earnings.

- His office is always buried in paper; yellow reminder stickers are plastered over his computer screen and wall.

- He is always "behind the eight ball" in terms of collecting money from his clients.

- He rarely finishes one task before beginning another.

- Although he has a contact management software system on his computer with most of his clients and prospects loaded into it, he does not bother keeping the information up-to-date. He does not want to take the time while making phone calls to update the information on the OTDB. As a result, he is forced to try (he rarely has the time to get to it) to update his OTDB database during the weekends or evenings.

I have known this gentleman for over 10 years. I can honestly say that he does not intend to be in a constant state of crisis. But he does not realize how he creates more work for himself by leaving loose ends. For instance, in the above example he has the sales management software that could help him organize his sales efforts. But because he feels rushed, he does not take the time to update his system while he is making follow-up calls. As a result, the benefits of automation are lost because he does not use the computer to remind him of the critical calls or tasks he has committed to, or take advantage of the software to keep track of important information on his clients or prospects. (He takes notes on paper that are little better than useless.)

The lesson I have learned from observing this fellow over the years is to slow down and do it right the first time, and, never, ever leave loose ends, for they certainly will come back to haunt me.

Summary

Before we list the software features and functions needed to utilize the concepts elaborated in this chapter, let's review what we have learned.

1. The only time you can make a sale is when you are in contact with an OTDB. Typically, there are only specific times during the day and week when you have the opportunity to contact an OTDB. It therefore makes common sense to plan your investment in time to maximize these contacts.

2. The Secret of Efficiency: *Do What You Do, When You Are Doing It!*

3. When using a contact management software system, it is essential you follow this practice: touch it once. If a good part of your day is spent selling on the phone, it is essential you have a software system that allows you to easily and quickly update your contact information *while you are on the phone.* When you hang up the phone, you need to have completed your data input.

Software Features Checklist

1. **Minimal keystrokes to input critical data.**

   The software must enable you to input critical data in an easy and efficient manner. This feature is important if you are going to update your OTDB database while on the phone with your contact.

   Required Software Functions:

   - Pop-up windows that allow you to pre-define input (e.g., lead source, business type, user-defined fields).

   - Pop-up calendar to simplify selecting and inputing of dates for scheduling calls, meetings, tasks, and other activities.

   - Hot keys to jump to critical screens (eliminate going through multiple menus to reach certain information).

   - Keyboard macros that allow multiple keyboard entries to be recorded and executed by hitting one key (typically, a function key on the keyboard).

2. **Ability to search for information by any field in the database.**

   You will need to find information, based upon various criteria, in your OTDB database quickly. You may want to locate OTDBs by their company name, phone number, main contact name, user-defined fields, or by any other data you have in your system. Cold calling and direct-mail campaigns often are based on industry and geographic locations (for instance, city, zip code, state—sorted by SIC code or business type). Finding information easily and quickly is one of the key productivity improvements you can achieve.

Required Software Functions:

- Quick-find or fast-find menu option that enables a user to input alpha information to locate a specific record (e.g., you want to find Joe Thompson in your database because he is returning your call; you need to search on the field that contains main contact names and input "Joe Thompson" to quickly pull up his OTDB data). The quick-find fields are called indexed fields. They enable the program to find information faster than sequentially searching through every record in your database.

- Ability to define "filters" to screen the information you see on the screen. For instance, if you want to locate all the distributors in your database who are located in New York, you need the capability to define this criteria (or filter) and sort quickly to locate these OTDBs.

- Ability to save filters or criteria, per above explanation, to be reused. This feature allows you to save your filters and select them from a pop-up window to use on demand (e.g., you can name your filters—in the previous example we could name it "distributors in NY"—so you don't have to redefine them every time you want to use them).

- System allows you to select filter criteria from any field of data in your system.

3. **Ability to make mass changes in your database.**

   There are occasions where you need to make mass changes to your OTDB database; for instance, if a salesperson is replaced by a new salesperson, you may want to change all the old salesperson's accounts (change the salesperson field from the old one to the new) via a global change. This saves a great deal of time over updating each OTDB record one at a time. (You may have hundreds of records.)

Required Software Function:

- Menu selection criteria that enables you to define which records should be changed and how (e.g., all records where salesperson = Jon Smith change to salesperson = Betty Bop).

4. **Automatic dialing of phone and tracking of time spent on call.**

Some contact management systems allow the computer to dial your phone. You need to have the computer attached to your phone via a modem. You select the OTDB you want to call, and which contact you wish to call, and the computer dials the number. These systems usually also track the amount of time you spent on the phone call and records this data in a history file.

Required Software Functions:

- Automatic dialing menu selection on system that notifies you when a phone connection is made.

- Menu that allows selection of contact you wish to call along with fields containing contact name and phone number.

- System default setup to define long-distance numbers and codes to work properly with your phone system. (Some companies have codes such as 9, 212, area code, phone number that are required to use their phone system.)

- History file that gets updated upon completion of call. Salesperson, OTDB company name, contact name, objective of call, results of call, and length of call are typical fields that get updated in the history file.

5. *Ad hoc* **report writer.**

Report writers enable users to create their own reports based on data in their OTDB database and various sorting criteria. Report writers can be useful if management requests non-standard reports that otherwise you would have to create manually. Some *ad hoc* report writers are difficult to learn to use, and others don't allow for sophisticated sorting or data manipulation and therefore are only marginally useful. The major advantage of *ad hoc* report writers is their ability to allow you to customize reports without modifying the software (and incurring the costs of programmers). Most report writers also allow you to create reports that you send to your disk drive (as opposed to a printer). The report data that is sent to the disk drive can then be loaded into a spreadsheet or relational database and manipulated with these tools.

Required Software Functions:

- A report writer that has been integrated with your sales management software data structure. The report writer needs to be connected to the fields in your OTDB database so that the two programs can work together. Some sales management programs use their own *ad hoc* report writers. Others use other companies' products that they have integrated into their sales management program.

- The report writer should output the data to a printer, disk, or your display. You should be able to select the output destination at the time of printing.

6. **On-line help available on demand.**

On-line help enables you to pull up user documentation on your screen. The system should pull up the section of the manual that relates to where you are in the software. (For example, if you are in the free-form notes field and you forgot how to save the notes, you hit a system-defined key, and the system brings up the documentation relating to free-form notes.). On-line help is useful when you originally begin using the software or when you are training new users.

Required Software Functions:

- On-line help menu that is enabled by pushing a function key or a series of keystrokes (e.g., control key and H).

- Ability to pull up an index of help topics to select section of documentation to review.

- **OPTIONAL:** ability to customize the help notes. Some systems allow you to put in the help descriptions you want. For instance, if you are using a particular numbering scheme to denote customers, you can change the on-line help screen to describe the manner in which you want to define customers' numbers.

Any feature of the software that helps you do your job faster, with fewer mistakes, will enable you to work smarter and thereby be more productive. And that is what making time work for you is all about.

Chapter 7

MANAGEMENT'S PERSPECTIVE— ISSUES TO CONSIDER

The purpose of this chapter is to elaborate on the special considerations and issues that automating the sales process will have on management as well as on the overall business. Depending on your industry and business circumstances, automating your salespeople and customer service representatives creates special opportunities and problems that need to be resolved in order to be successful.

Management Issues to Check

Clear Objectives

Management must set clear objectives and determine the critical issues to manage (track).

Management must have clear objectives for automating their sales force and processes. They also must develop a game plan that lays out the steps required to accomplish the objectives. The firm's payback needs to be determined so that management can cost-justify the effort required to carry out their plans effectively.

One common mistake management makes when automating their sales force is to not clearly define their goals and objectives. They simply purchase a contact management software package for their salespeople and give it to them. Each salesperson utilizes the software tool (or doesn't use it at all) according to their own interest and whims. Corporate benefits from this approach are minimal at best, and most salespeople's productivity gains are marginal.

Involve Salespeople with Selection and Implementation

Management must approach their salespeople from the perspective of helping them make more money (via improved productivity, customer service, etc.), as opposed to the "Big Brother" syndrome of management snooping.

It is critical that your salespeople are an integral part of the planning and implementation process. You will have little chance of success if your sales force does not see how they will benefit from using the tools (technology) you are providing them.

On the other hand, recognize the tendency of people to fear change. I suggest you use the carrot and the stick approach with your sales staff. The "carrot" is the elimination of paperwork, improvement of productivity that will lead to greater rewards, and overall benefits they will realize by using contact management systems effectively. The "stick" is the insistence by upper management that all salespeople adhere to the policies and practices required to use this technology. Remember to reward the behavior you want your sales staff to practice.

One of the most important ingredients for using computer systems successfully, especially for salespeople, is discipline. If you use the technology day in and day out, you will receive the payback. Management must set clear policies that make sense, and then ensure they are followed.

Define Critical Information Needed

Management must define the critical information needed to capture and track customers, prospects, dealers, and so on. Management needs to pre-define how this information should be categorized so it will be useful (consistent data input).

Computer systems, by their nature, are dumb; they only do exactly what you tell them to. The following are examples of information that needs to be pre-defined to be useful:

- Lead Source: It is important to know where your business is coming from. You must determine the appropriate means of defining your lead sources so that your salespeople are consistent in how they input this information. (See Figure 7–1)

- Progress Level: If you want to keep track of your OTDBs in your sales pipeline, you need to define the steps in your sales cycle so that all salespeople share definitions. (See Figure 7–2.)

- Business Type: Most businesses want to analyze their clients and OTDBs by SIC code or industry type. Again, consistent definitions are required. (See Figure 7–3.)

- User-Defined Information: Most contact management software allows for user-defined fields to customize the information being captured. Examples of user-defined fields are customer interest, competition, and product/service targeted to sell. (See Figure 7–4.)

Figure 7–1   Sample Pop-Up Window on Lead Source

```
CONTACT
Goto  Track  Agenda  Edit  Dial  Plan  Letter  Order  View  Script  Report  Quit
Select and/or run a script
```

```
Company Interactive                 Phone        Ext       Time/Date
Contact John Overend                (708) 490-9600         10:39A L
Title   VP                          (800) 451-1646         06/15/93
Dear:   John
Address 2401 Hassell rd             AcctExec Jon C. Liberman
        Suite 1500                  BusType  Service
City    Hoffman Estates      S ate IL  Progress C - Referral  ource
                          ?ate 04 21/93 :
Source  Personal/JCL            ther/Crains                ate  /  /
                                 ersonal/
                                 ersonal/JCL
06/14/93 - John AST problem  was ersonal/Nicki Weber       l -
06/03/93 - Tim Scheele has lead  ersonal/Ruth Weiner       ramming -
05/20/93 - Hillary, 5% of dealer ersonal/Stacey Kahan      nal 5% for
Ontario -                        eminars/CPA Trade Show 87
04/28/93 - John, (I need Sifa qu elemarketing/5/6/91       'll call me
tommorrow                        elemarketing/Matrix Group
                                 elemarketing/T. Wilkins
```

                    DY-Select   Backspace-Clear

Who Needs Access to the System?

Management must determine who needs to share access to the database of information. For example, do multiple people or departments need to access and update information on a particular customer?

If your organization is going to need to share information with other people or departments, management needs to make sure the software can accommodate these requirements. For instance, if your business involves inside and outside salespeople

Figure 7–2   Screen Showing Progress Level of Sales Pipeline

```
TRACK
Contact  Results  Task  DoneTask  NextDate  Failed  Progress  ViewHistory  Quit
Update progress code

Company Interactive                        Phone      Ext      Time/Date
Contact John Overend                       (708) 490-9600       10:08A L
Title   VP                                 (800) 451-1646       06/15/93
Dear:   John
Address 2401 Hassell rd                    AcctExec Jon C. Liberman
        Suite 1500                         Bus
City    Hoffman Estates   State IL         Pro  0 – Suspect
Country USA          Zip 60195             Rat  1 – Initial Contact
Source  Personal/JCL                       Pot  2 – Qualifying
                                                3 – Fact Finding
                                                4 – Proposal
TRACKING                                        5 – Presentation/Demo
                                                6 – Ask to buy
Last Contact  Call                   Next  7 – Active Client Project
When Completed 06/14/93  2:28P  :    When  8 – Client – new opportunity
Last Objective F/U Musikantow AST    Next  9 – Inactive Client
Results       Completed               Prior

Last Attempt     /  /    12:00A      Next
Reason Failed                        When Due      /  /      12:00P
                                     Priority

                      DY-Select  Backspace-Clear
```

Figure 7–3   Sample Pop-Up Window on Business Type

```
CONTACT
Goto  Track  Agenda  Edit  Dial  Plan  Letter  Order  View  Script  Report  Quit
Select and/or run a script
```

```
Company Interactive                    Phone          Ext        Time/Date
Contact John Overend                   (708) 490-9600            10:39A L
Title   VP                             (800) 451-1646            06/15/93
Dear:   John
Address 2401 Hassell rd                Acc
        Suite 1500                     Bus  Association/1 - Trade Assoc
City    Hoffman Estates     State IL   Pro  Association/2 - Social Service
Country USA         Zip 60195          Rat  Construction
Source  Personal/JCL                   Pot  Dist
                                            Dist/1 - Food              M
NOTES                                       Dist/2 - Plastic           D
06/14/93 - John AST problem was with setup  Education
06/03/93 - Tim Scheele has lead for me; Been Finance
05/20/93 - Hillary, 5% of dealer value = 1st Finance/1 - Commodities
Ontario -                                   Finance/2 - Venture Capital
04/28/93 - John, (I need Sifa quote); will
tommorrow
```

DY-Select Backspace-Clear

working accounts together, they need to have access to the same information.

This can lead to problems if your software only allows for database updating by overwriting the data. Overwriting the data means one user (e.g., an outside salesperson with a laptop computer) communicates his or her information (via modem over the phone, by diskette, etc.) to a central office database. The remote user copies his or her records (e.g., a prospect named ACME CO.) and overwrites (copies over the ACME CO. record in the central database with the new ACME record from the remote data). If

Figure 7–4   Sample User-Defined Fields

```
CONTACT
Goto  Track  Agenda  Edit  Dial  Plan  Letter  Order  View  Script  Report  Quit
Select and/or run a script
```

```
Company James E. Van Ella              Phone        Ext       Time/Date
Contact Laura Bibergall                (312) 693-6220          10:42A L
Title   Executive Vice President       (312) 693-7356 FAX      06/15/93
Dear:   Laura
Address 8420 W. Brwyn Mawr             AcctExec Jon C. Liberman
        Suite # 200                    BusType  Service
City    Chicago            State IL    Progress 4 - Proposal
Country USA           Zip 60638        Rating   80% Origin Date 06/25/90
Source  Vendor/PCD-Debbie             Potential $   15000 Date 07/31/93

USER DEFINED
Opersys    Novell                    Interest3
Hardware   LAN-Ethernet              Size_users
Hardware2                            Niche       Detective Agency
Software1  Customized by Martoccio   Competitor  Intelligent Solutions
Software2  Rbase custom soft         Locations
Software3                            Buying_Phs
Interest1                            Maintagre  No
Interest2                            Date_FUM15  /  /

Record 120    of 541    Index Company   Filter OFF            Call OFF
```

your inside salesperson has notes from a conversation that occurred previous to the data communication, it will be erased by
the new record from the outside salesperson.

This aspect of contact management systems is one of the most
complex. If you require multiple sharing of client or prospect
information, you must determine exactly how the system must
work to accomplish your objectives. Several possible scenarios for
sharing sales management information exist:

1. Remote users update home offices via modem commu-
    nications. Remote sales offices or salespeople on the road

maintain their own OTDB databases and pass management information to the central office on a regular basis (daily, weekly, etc.).

Required Software Capabilities:

- Export ability in software to create data file containing required data (general ID information, agenda information, electronic notes, user-defined information, etc.).

- Import ability in software to load exported data file into corporate database.

- If you require the software not to overwrite the database (per the example in #4), the software needs to append the newly updated information to the existing database. Appending the information requires the system to "flag" the database every time the salesperson (or remote office) exports their data. The software keeps track of all the information that changes in the database; only the changes are exported.

- You will require a communications software package to facilitate the physical hook-up between your remote users passing information over the phone lines, via a modem, and the home system. Most of the contact management packages available can work with most of the popular off-the-shelf packages available (such as Carbon Copy, PC Anywhere, and Procom Plus).

2. Multiple users in one office share software and information via a local area network. (See Figure 7–5.)

Required Software Capabilities:

- The sales management software you will be using must be compatible with the networking scheme you will be using (Novell, Lantastic, etc.). You need the

Figure 7–5   Diagram of LAN

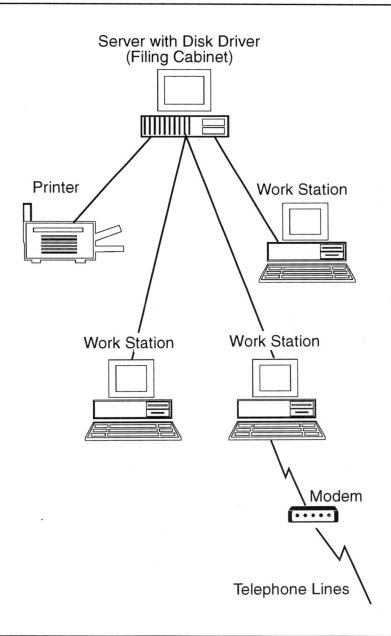

Server with Disk Driver
(Filing Cabinet)

Printer

Work Station

Work Station

Work Station

Modem

Telephone Lines

software to provide record locking protection. Record locking means the software allows one user to access a specific record of information at one time (e.g., when ACME CO. is being accessed by one user, no other users can update that record until the first user is finished). You need record locking because if two users update the same record at the same time, the computer will lose the data. (Lost data typically is called corrupted data in computerese).

NOTE: You will require record locking to use contact management software effectively on a network. You typically do not want file locking in the software because it usually is not practical. (File locking locks out the whole file of information when a user is accessing one record in the file.) If you load single-user software on a network, and the software has not been designed to run on the LAN with record-locking capabilities, the software typically will not function properly.

3. Multiple users in one office use a LAN, plus remote users (sales offices and outside salespeople) access the system, with all sharing data. (See Figure 7–6.)

Required Software Capabilities:

- All of the features discussed in 1 and 2 apply.

- Communications with remote users and the home office LAN may require special software and hardware products. The critical issues revolve around the number of remote users needing concurrent access, the type of networking scheme being used, and the amount of data being transferred. I recommend you utilize computer knowledgeable people (either internal staff or outside consultants) to help you in this area.

NOTE: If your business objectives necessitate multiple offices with internal and outside salespeople needing to communicate, I strongly suggest you get professional help in

Figure 7–6   Diagram of LAN with Remote Users

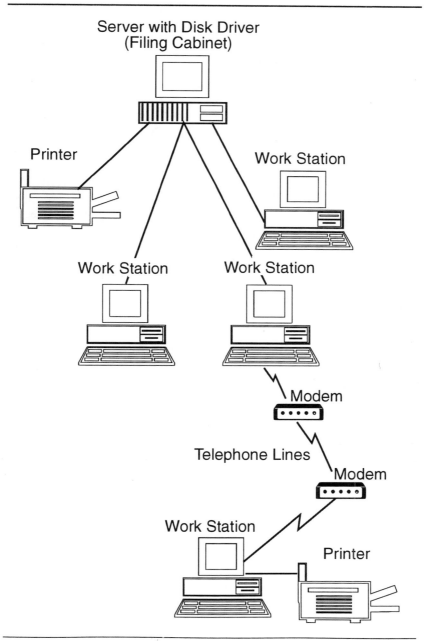

selecting and implementing an automated solution. Many issues affecting the usefulness and costs exist, but are beyond the scope of this book.

Security Requirements

Management must determine what the security requirements are for allowing updating and inquiry into the database.

What level of security do you need the software to handle to protect access to sensitive information? Most software provides for password protection, which means if you type in the correct password, you have access to everything in your database. Some systems allow you to set up different databases for each salesperson, so they can't have access to other salespeople's information. This approach limits sharing of information and can become unwieldy.

Some systems allow for several levels of security. Each user on the system is given a password and a user rating. The user rating determines the programs and data to which they have access. In some programs the user ratings determine if the user can update (change information) or only inquire (look at but not change). Management must resolve how they need the system to function prior to selecting a software system. Again, if your requirements become somewhat sophisticated, I recommend you get professional assistance.

Enterprise-wide automation can provide tremendous competitive advantages for some businesses. The issues involved in selecting and implementing an automated system that will be used by your sales force, marketing management, customer service staff, engineers, and so on to manage all of your selling and servicing functions is beyond the scope of this book. This book is primarily concerned with automating your selling, service, and marketing functions as they relate to your sales force and management.

Case Study: Small Distributor Automates Sales Force

This case study will detail the process one small business experienced when it decided to automate its sales force. The business is a privately-owned distributor of paper and plastic packaging to manufacturers, airlines, food processors, and other related businesses. They have one warehouse/headquarters and one small remote sales office. They have a customer base of 300 active clients as well as approximately 1,500 prospects that they pursue. All together they have nine salespeople.

The Company Seeks Help

The owner of this business approached his accounting firm, who had provided computer systems consulting and implementation assistance when they automated their accounting/order processing/inventory management systems, to see if they could help. His CPA firm had a consultant who used sales management software and had assisted several other firms successfully to automate their sales forces.

The client asked the consultant to meet with the owner, his management team and sales force to discuss their goals and review the software that the consultant had employed previously. They were unsure as to the best approach available to them. Should they look for a PC-based sales management package or try to develop something using a database package that someone on their staff was familiar with? They had installed a Novell network several months earlier to run word processing and spreadsheet packages, and thought that, in either case, they would run the software on this network.

In the meeting between the consultant and client, they reviewed the software the consultant used on his laptop computer. The client had not developed any requirements lists or even written down any concrete objectives. This is very typical. The consultant began by helping them define their objectives.

Their objectives for automating were three-fold:

1. To improve the productivity of their salespeople by auto-mating their client and prospect follow-up, mailings, and management reporting functions.

2. To improve their company's marketing effectiveness by automating their OTDB database with demographic and client purchase-related information. They wanted to be able to track client-specific purchasing and competitive information and sort by "customer type" classifications, so that they could "rifle" target their calling campaigns and react to opportunities as they came up.

3. To gain better control over their OTDB database. They had experienced turnover of their sales force and lost contact with some of the accounts those people had worked with.

A Sales Management Software Package Is Selected

It was decided that attempting to customize a system in a database program would be too expensive and too difficult because no one on the client's staff had the expertise to design a viable system without a great deal of trial and error. The "trial and error" approach to custom programming is very expensive and takes a long time to finally produce a working system. The package that the consultant used and demonstrated to the client seemed to be an easy way to get started. The package would accommodate the basic functions the client wanted to automate, was relatively inexpensive, and allowed for multiple user-defined fields, which would allow the client to capture the industry-specific informa-tion they needed. It also worked with the word processing soft-ware they were running on their LAN. The major advantage the package had for the client was the fact that the consultant they trusted was thoroughly familiar with it and as a result could help them figure out how to use it to accomplish their objectives.

A Steering Committee Is Formed

The first step the consultant recommended to his client was to form a client steering committee. The steering committee would be responsible for developing a list of their company's system requirements, reviewing the project's timetable and status, assigning people tasks, and ensuring overall project success. The committee was made up of the owner (president), the controller, the systems administrator (who ran the computers for the firm), the sales manager, and three salespeople. One of the sales staff had some experience with sales management software; none of the rest of the sales staff had any experience with computers at all.

The client's sales force spent a good deal of their time in the field visiting clients and prospects. As a result, it was decided that each salesperson would get a laptop computer to manage their OTDB database and download their information into the LAN. The corporate OTDB database would be maintained on the LAN system. The downloading would initially be accomplished via diskettes (data would be copied from laptop to diskette and the diskette uploaded onto the LAN), but at a later date, when all the kinks were worked out, modem communications would be added to allow the salespeople phone downloading capabilities. The client ordered the required software and hardware.

A Pilot Project Is Started

The four salespeople (including the manager) who were part of the steering committee would pilot the project. They would be the first users of the software and would work out any kinks prior to attempting to get all the rest of the sales staff up and running.

The consultant scheduled a kick-off meeting with the steering committee. In the kick-off meeting the consultant reviewed the objectives for the project and discussed what critical data elements they would need to define in order to capture the information necessary to accomplish their business objectives. The consultant suggested that the client work backwards to figure out what their critical data was. For instance, what critical reports would management need from the salespeople ? How would management and the salespeople need to find / locate information in the system? Once they had determined the end results they needed, they could figure out (with the consultant's help) what information they would need to track to create the required end result. The steering committee determined the critical end results and was able to define the critical data elements they needed to capture. In several cases the data elements needed to be pre-defined as to the appropriate inputs to ensure all nine users consistently defined things in the same manner. Examples of critical data elements needing to be pre-defined were the progress field, to track the sales pipeline; the products purchased field, to define the product categories the OTDBs purchase; and the competitors field, to track who the client was competing with.

The software was installed on the client's LAN and on the pilot participants' laptops. The original training session was held with the consultant reviewing the software with the steering committee in the conference room. Homework was assigned to each member of the pilot group, and additional training was handled via the phone or on a one-on-one basis as needed. The salesperson who had previous experience had no difficulty using the system from day one. He had occasional questions that could be answered by the consultant over the phone. The inexperienced salespeople needed more hand-holding by the consultant. But, after two to three weeks of using the software to schedule calls, update notes, and manage their daily activities, they were up and running smoothly. Several quirks or bugs in the software were discovered during the first three weeks but nothing that caused the pilot project to suffer complications. After four weeks, the typical response from the sales force was disbelief that they had ever functioned without it. Once they established the habit of using the computer, they discovered how useful it had become to them.

The steering committee reviewed the status of the project on a biweekly basis for the first six weeks. After this time they decided that several changes were required to the user-defined fields and internal procedures to improve the system's performance. They also decided that the rest of the sales force should be installed.

Implementation Is Complete

The client had assigned one of the salespeople who was involved in the pilot project to train the other salespeople in the firm with backup from the consultant as needed. It took the firm a total of three months from initial installation to be functioning on the system. They were not utilizing all the capabilities of the software at this time, but had successfully implemented the basics of agenda management, tracking activities, performing mailings, and managing their OTDB database. The system is not static. They are continually making little changes and have used the report-writing capabilities to create more meaningful reports. They also have determined that, at a future date, they may wish to modify the basic package to enhance its usefulness. But, all in all, they have put in place the infrastructure they need to accomplish their objectives.

Summary

Before we list the software features and functions needed to utilize the concepts elaborated in Chapter 7, let's review what we have learned:

1. Management must set clear objectives and determine the critical issues to manage (track).

2. Management must approach their salespeople from the perspective of helping them make more money (via improved productivity, customer service, etc.) as opposed to the "Big Brother" syndrome of management snooping.

3. Management must define the critical information needed to capture and track customers, prospects, dealers, etc. Management will need to pre-define how this informa-

tion needs to be categorized so as to be useful when management is analyzing the information (consistent data input).

4. Management must determine who needs to share access to the database of information. Do multiple people or departments need to access and update information on a particular customer, etc.?

5. Management must determine the security requirements for allowing updating and inquiry into the database.

Software Features Checklist

To successfully utilize a computer system to automate your sales and marketing functions, the following features may be necessary:

1. Required data entry fields are useful when you need the information to be captured in your OTDB database. For instance, tracking the lead source of your business is important. If you set up this field to be a required field, whenever the record is set up, the cursor will not move to the next field without an entry of information. If you also use pop-up windows with pre-defined input, you can ensure consistent and accurate information in critical fields.

   Required Software Functions:

   • Required fields are either system-set (the software comes with the fields set up as required), or user-defined. Some systems allow a user-defined field to be set with a required field attribute.

   • Pop-up window with pre-defined items.

2. Telemarketing scripts with multiple branches can be useful for telemarketing operations, customer surveying,

and cold-calling campaigns. The software needs to enable you to create the scripts and link (branch) responses for easy flow.

Required Software Functions:

- Telemarketing scripts with menu capability to link to multiple branches (or screen responses).

- Ability to create script screens (similar to word processing documents) and save script with unique code or name. System must provide capability to link script codes into branching menu.

3. Management must determine the security requirements for allowing updating and inquiry into the database. What level of security do you need the software to handle to protect access to sensitive information?

Required Software Functions:

- Password protection based on log-in name (for example, the name you logged into the computer under your salesman code); if you type in the correct password, you have access to everything in your database. Some systems allow you to set up different databases for each salesperson so that they cannot have access to other salespeople's information. This approach limits sharing of information and can become cumbersome.

- Password and user rating, controlling levels of access. Each user on the system is given a password and a user rating. The user rating determines the programs and data to which they can have access. In some programs the user ratings can determine if the user can update (change information) or only inquire (look at but not change).

4. Multi-user/sharing information requirements. If you need multiple people to share information or computing

resources, you will need a multi-user hardware and software system. You need the software to provide record locking protection. Record locking means the software allows one user to access a specific record of information at a time. You need record locking because if two users update the same record at the same time, the computer will "lose" the data (called corrupted data in computerese). Several types of multi-user systems are available. The most popular in the PC world are either Local Area Networking (LAN) or UNIX (from AT&T) systems.

Required Software Functions:

- The sales management software you will be using must be compatible with the multi-user scheme you will be using. Examples of multi-user schemes for LANs include Novell, Lantastic, and so on.

- Print spooler capabilities provide the ability to send a report to a print spooler on the disk instead of directly to a printer. This is useful if a printer is being shared by several users and you do not want to tie up your system waiting for the printer to free up, or if you want to load special forms or paper and wish to print all your reports at once.

5. Communication data importing/exporting capabilities. If you are going to need to import data (bring data in from another computer system) or export data (send data to another computer system), you need the software to provide distributed communications capabilities.

Required Software Functions:

- You need the software to import and export data in standard data formats so that they can easily interface with other programs. Standard data formats include ASCII, dBase, and a host of others. You must make certain of compatibility with any other software you want to communicate with.

- If you are communicating with your own sales force via modem or diskette, you need the system to allow for exporting and importing of OTDB database, history, and notes information.

- You must determine if overwriting of the OTDB database, history files, or notes information is going to cause a problem. Typically, you need the notes and history files to be appended to the record in the receiving system, as opposed to overwriting the record.

- You will require a communications software package to facilitate the physical hook-up between your remote users, who are passing information over the phone lines via a modem, and the home system. Most of the contact management packages available can work with most of the popular off-the-shelf packages available (such as Carbon Copy, PC Anywhere, Procom Plus).

NOTE: If your business objectives necessitate multiple offices with internal and outside salespeople needing to communicate with each other, we strongly suggest you use professional help in selecting and implementing an automated solution.

6. Systems "housekeeping" functions are necessary to maximize productivity, keep the sales management system running properly, and protect your data.

Required Software Functions:

- Data backup capability is essential to protect your OTDB assets and information stored in the computer. All computer systems provide for backup of some sort.

- Data corruption housekeeping. You need the software to automatically rebuild any files that may get corrupted. Re-indexing functions will clean up corrupted files and usually help the system run faster.

- Purging of historical and notes data from your database on somewhat of a regular basis is necessary. The size of your computer's hard drive will determine how much historical and notes information you can store on your computer. You need to selectively purge your database of certain information. Purging options include by date (delete all history after a selected date for all records) and by account (which allows for selected history to be deleted on an account-by-account or record-by-record basis).

- Indexing fields of information (such as company name) enables the software to find information faster than having to go through each record sequentially to find what you want. You need to make sure that any critical information you will need to locate in the system is an indexed field, or, as your database grows, your system will become slower.

- Duplicate record checking checks if a prospect you are entering is already in your system.

- **OPTIONAL:** Pop-up calculator, The ability to hit a function key on your keyboard and access a calculator on your screen. The calculator pops up in a window and can input the calculation into the data field you were in when you popped up the calculator.

- On-line help provides the user documentation at the touch of a button. The system will provide context-sensitive help based upon the field the cursor is on when you hit the help key.

- On-line systems documentation provides on-line systems information such as amount of disk space available, version of the software, current database logged into, and so forth.

- DOS Hot Key allows for a user to hit a "hot key" (function key or combination of two keys) to exit the contact management system and go into the operating system to access another program; when finished, hit another hot key to be back in the contact management system in the same place from which you exited. (NOTE: Microsoft Windows and MAC applications perform this function without the need for "hot keys.")

- Copy Record function allows a user to copy data from one record to another and then make the desired changes to the new record. This can save time if you are loading a number of records with similar information and only want to change a few fields, such as contact name or phone number.

- Send Reports to the screen or disk allows the user, when printing, to send the report to the screen to review (thereby saving paper) or to your hard disk so that you can load the data into a spreadsheet or database program (provides another way to link with other systems).

7. Operating system options for the micro computer. Software has to be designed to work with a particular operating system inorder to run properly. Several standard operating systems exist for microcomputers. Our focus has been on the most popular options, including the following:

- IBM or Microsoft DOS, known as DOS. DOS provides for single-user operation only. (Only one user can use the system and access the data at a time.)

- Windows from Microsoft. Windows runs "on top of" DOS and provides for graphical interface with the software and uses mouse input along with the keyboard. The Macintosh computer line from Apple works in the same fashion, only under the MAC operating system. They both make the software easier to use.

- Novell networking is the most popular means of connecting single-user DOS or Window computers into a Local Area Network. Record locking, print spooling, and improved security are several capabilities Novell provides.

- Unix software, from AT&T, provides multi-user capabilities. Unix systems typically have a main computer (known as a "server") that terminals can be attached to in order to share programs, data, and printers.

The next chapter, Determining What To Automate, will help you organize all of your software requirements and determine what you need.

Chapter 8

DETERMINING WHAT TO AUTOMATE

This chapter will integrate all the lessons and software requirements covered in the previous chapters. The focus of this chapter
is to help you determine what aspects of your marketing and sales
process you should automate and what software features you will
require to successfully accomplish your objectives.

The first question you need to ask yourself in order to determine what to automate is What's the payback?

For example, the benefits of automating your phone follow-
up process might be minimal if you spend the majority of your
time in face-to-face meetings with clients. On the other hand, if
you spend the majority of your time on the phone, automated

callbacks will provide excellent benefits and should be one of the first areas you computerize.

You need to think about your sales process and relate the benefits against the cost (money plus time) of each functional area that a computer might automate. The following examples will aid you in determining what the payback would be.

Payback from the Salesperson's Perspective

The critical payback from a salesperson's perspective involves bottom-line, improved productivity that will lead to increased sales. As mentioned in previous chapters, as salespeople we can make sales only when we are in contact with OTDBs. Sales automation software can improve your productivity with the following capabilities:

1. Agenda follow-up management

   • Schedule calls, meetings, tasks, etc.

   • Daily "to-do lists" and calls are sorted by priority.

   • Automatic alarms notify you of critical to-do's.

2. Instant inquiry into your OTDB database

   • Find information immediately through index inquiries by phone number, company name, contact name, user-defined information, etc.

   • Locate OTDBs who meet certain criteria such as industry, geographic location, product/services purchased, and competitors used.

3. Improved personalized service

   • Use the free-form notes fields to remind you of conversations and important details.

- Use the notes fields to communicate with customer service staff or other people you work with on your accounts.

- Use the integrated word processor to easily send personalized notes and letters to keep in touch with OTDBs and clients.

4. Minimized administrative work

- Produce projected sales reports on demand.

- Create activity reports for any period of time.

- Satisfy management reporting requirements with a touch of a button.

5. Easily produced proposals and quotations

- Word processing can print proposals or quotes with minimal effort.

- Fax quotes/proposals via the phone with automated fax hardware and software.

- Utilize direct-mail campaigns to generate leads via mailing lists integrated with word processors and form letters.

Payback from Management's Perspective

The critical payback from management's perspective involves improving their salespeople's productivity (as described above), improving marketing effectiveness and OTDB continuity (managing the OTDBs as an asset of the business), and overall improved customer service. Sales automation software can provide these benefits with the following capabilities:

1. Managing the sales pipeline to ensure consistent results

- Track the progress of your OTDBs through your sales cycles.

- Measure market plans and campaign effectiveness by tracking lead source numbers (number of suspects fed into pipeline, actual revenue by lead source, etc.).

- Assist sales management in coaching sales staff by evaluating their sales pipeline trends over time.

2. Improved marketing effectiveness via database management of critical information

- Locate OTDBs who fit specific characteristics for direct-mail or telemarketing.

- Manage marketing plans by automating each step (e.g., first step: send form letter #1; second step: call after seven days to determine interest; third step: send client testimonials, etc.) and tracking results. (See Figures 8–1 and 8–2.)

- Manage quotation/proposal process and ensure timely follow-up by automating proposal production and scheduled follow-up.

- Evaluate marketing and sales performance by tracking trends and budget to actual results for marketing plans, product lines, region/territories, and sales person.

3. Improved control and management of your OTDB assets

- Eliminate the potential loss of OTDB assets when salespeople leave by maintaining the OTDB database at your home office.

- Manage salespeople follow-up by tracking their activity via activity reports.

4. Improved customer service

- Track customer commitments and communications by using automated notes fields and follow-up tracking mechanisms.

Figure 8-1   Screen Showing Step Four of Marketing Plan

```
File  Edit  Members  Report  Help                        10:26:03 am
                         Action Plan

Plan Name COMDEX 92 LEADS                     Starting Date 11/01/92

                         Steps in the Plan

Step:  4

Objective of this step:  Close Sale

( ) Call
( ) Meeting
( ) Task      <Letter...>

Progress level contact must be at for this step:  6 - Ask To Buy

Schedule this step  0 days ( ) from last action ( ) from start date

. Edit /   <Delete>    < New >    < Next >    <Prior >    <Browse>
```

Figure 8-2   Screen Showing Steps in Marketing Plan

File Edit Members Report Help   10:25:29 am
                          Action Plan

Plan Name COMDEX 92 LEADS   Starting Date 11/01/92

Step: 1   Steps in the Plan

Obje   3Step Action Objective   Select a Step

                                                              3
   ( )   1   Call   Qualify
   ( )   2   Task   Send Literature Package
   ( )   3   Call   Follow up on Letter
              4   Meeting Close Sale
Prog

Schedule this step   0 days ( ) from last action ( ) from start date   3

      Edit /   <Delete>   < New >   < Next >   <Prior >   <Browse>

- Schedule regular customer contact and follow-up by using agenda management processes to schedule calls.

5. Increased leads

  - Use demographic and user profile information of database to target mailing campaigns.

  - Use agenda management automation to schedule regular contact of lead sources and Opportunities To Refer Business (client referrals, vendor leads, lawyer referrals, etc.).

  - Use telemarketing scripts to ensure consistent and professional message when soliciting for leads.

Regardless of the rationale you have for automating your sales and marketing processes, the following topic areas will help you organize your efforts and assist in determining what your software and system requirements will be. To aid in this process, please think about the following topics and determine the appropriate answers for you (and your firm). We have provided examples and rationales after each question to help you understand why the information is important and how to use it. We have included a Software Requirements form to help you respond to these topic areas. Feel free to make a photocopy of the requirements form for your own use.

You should get input from as many of the proposed users of the system as possible. This will minimize the chance that something important is missed and will be helpful once you begin implementing the new system.

Topic Areas: Determining What to Automate

1. **List the specific objectives you have for automating; in other words, what do you hope to accomplish by automating?**

This is the logical place to begin. Describe your objectives in as simple and straightforward a manner as possible. An example of one of my objectives is to use the tickler lists of my system to ensure that I don't miss any opportunities or forget calls or tasks needing to be done.

2. **In order to accomplish the objectives in #1 above, who will need to share information and computer resources?**

    If you are a salesperson who works on his or her own, you may only need a stand-alone computer or notebook system. On the other hand, if you are automating your entire office—which includes inside and outside salespeople—you may require a local area network with remote users downloading information. Look at the big picture and understand who will need to have access to the information. The following are several possible scenarios:

    - Stand alone with hard copy reports

    - LAN in office—share notes

    - Salespeople in the field and secretaries to handle mailings

    - Inside and outside salespeople needing to share information and notes

3. **List the steps in your sales pipeline.**

    What are the steps or phases involved in your sales process? You can't manage something you can't measure. Tracking the progress of your OTDBs through your sales pipeline will give you control over your selling process and enable you to be more proactive.

    What are the critical steps that a prospect takes—from the initial point of contact, through the qualifying stages, to the consumation of the relationship (they give you money)? If you pursue repeat business with your clients, the ongoing account management steps must be part of your sales pipeline. An example of my sales pipeline includes the following:

a. Suspect

b. Initial Contact

c. Qualifying

d. Fact Finding

e. Proposal

f. Presentation/Demonstration

g. Ask for the Business

h. Active Customer

i. New Opportunity—Client

j. Inactive Client

k. Lead Source

l. Vendor

4. **What critical information will you need to manage your sales pipeline?**

For instance, do you need to track the number of suspects fed into your pipeline for a specific product line, or do you need to track what your most profitable lead source is?

Use the objectives you defined in number one above as a checklist to ensure you have covered all the bases. In the objective I used (tickler system—drop no balls), I needed on-line inquires and reports that list out all my commitments daily (in terms of calls, meetings, tasks, etc.).

5. **What critical reports do you need?**

What information do you presently receive that helps you manage your business? What information would you want to receive, that you presently do not, that would be valuable? The reason that figuring out what information/reports you want to get out of your sales management system is important is that it defines the information that the system must capture in order to report it to you.

6. **Based upon your previous responses, determine the critical data elements you need to keep track of.**

   You need to think about critical data elements as a means to an end. The end is the business objectives you defined in #1. Looking at the results you hope to achieve (e.g., tickler system—drop no balls) provides the framework for what critical data elements you need your system to capture so as to be able to report and track them effectively. In the above example, I needed to track specific follow-up activities (phone call, task, meetings, letter, etc.) by date and priority.

7. **Do you need a contact management system that is linked with your present word processing software, or do you want the contact management software to provide the letter-writing capabilities?**

   Most contact management systems provide some ability to do word processing and form letters. Most businesses that use microcomputers are using one of the popular word processing packages. If you want to continue to use your stand-alone word processing software, you need to ensure that there is an easy way to pass the client information into your word processor so as to eliminate re-typing the information (company name and address, etc.).

8. **When you need to find information on a client or prospect, what are the indexes (or sorting criteria) you will need?**

For instance, you probably will need to find your information by company name, contact name, phone number, etc. Are there any unique or different ways you need to get at your critical information? Think about what you will need, when you are on the phone and a call is coming in, to quickly locate the correct information.

9. **Do you want to produce quotes for clients and track their progress?**

   If your business sends out written quotes, you may want the ability to prepare and print the quote from your contact management software. You need to make certain that the manner in which you determine pricing can be duplicated and managed by your software.

10. **Do you want to integrate order processing and sales history information with your quote and contact management system (see year-to-date sales while talking to the client on the phone, update the order processing system, etc.)?**

    Do you want to create orders automatically from your quotation system? If you do, you need the software to accommodate this easily, which usually involves some customization or finding a package that can process your orders.

    If you want to track year-to-date sales or profit information, you need the means of capturing this data or integrating with your business software to capture this information.

11. **Do you need the ability to create ad hoc reports on demand?**

    Ad hoc reporting can be very useful when the need to "massage" your database in a different or unique manner arises. Requests from management, or your clients, for information can sometimes only be easily resolved by creating an ad hoc report. One problem with *ad hoc* reporting software (commonly referred to as report writers) is that they require more advanced knowledge than most "non-technical" users have. As a result, they can be difficult and cumbersome to use.

12. **Do you want to track expenses for meals, mileage, etc.?**

Self-explanatory.

13. **Do you need the ability to electronically read into your system computerized databases of prospects, etc.?**

If you plan on using third-party lists and databases to update your database electronically, you must make certain your software can accommodate them. This can be a very tricky area. I suggest that if you do not have the knowledge of ASCII file importing/exporting, that you find someone who does to help you evaluate and implement your software.

14. **Do you need your system to check for duplicate records (to ensure the same prospect is not in the system twice)?**

For instance, checking the business phone number can identify duplicate numbers but not duplicate names. You may have a situation where several salespeople are calling on the same company but contacting different people with different phone numbers.

15. **What level of security will you need?**

Security can be another tricky area. Most packages provide for the use of password protection to access your database and software. Some business situations necessitate people being able to look but not change certain information, or to have access only to specific areas of use or information. Be clear on your security needs, and make sure the selected package satisfies them.

16. **Do you need the ability to use "filters" and bring up to the screen only those records (prospects) that meet certain criteria?**

This is useful in some cold calling campaigns or to locate prospects that fit certain criteria such as OTDBs in specific cities or industries, etc.

17. **Do you need to send faxes electronically?**

Do you want the software to fax documents or correspondence to clients electronically via the computer? This feature can save time because no one needs to touch any paper—the computer dials the phone and sends the fax automatically.

18. **Do you want the computer to automatically dial the phone number of the person you are calling?**

Some systems can automatically dial your phone and track the amount of time spent on each call. If you bill for your time, and spend a good deal of time on the phone, this may be useful.

19. **Will you utilize telemarketers who will use interactive scripts with branching responses?**

If you need the contact management system to handle telemarketing scripts with branching responses, be careful to ensure it will meet your requirements. I suggest you let the telemarketers test out the software prior to purchase in order to ensure your expectations are met.

20. **Do you need two-way communications with your sales staff (send and receive information versus send only)?**

If you want to send electronic mail or other information to remote salespeople or regional offices, you need to make certain the software works the way you need it to work.

21. **Do you need to pre-define certain data input to ensure consistency throughout your system.**

For instance, if you need to track the source of your leads and have multiple sales staff, you need to have pre-defined input defining the possible lead sources (e.g., Comdex 93 trade show, *Business Week* ad, etc.) so that everyone is inputting the same lead source in a consistent manner.

22. **Do you need to track your sales process by market segments or market plans?**

    Automated market plans can be very useful in managing mailing campaigns and telemarketing efforts. Do you want to set up certain prospects (or suspects) in a multi-step plan that ensures the appropriate contact? For instance, the first step may involve sending a specific form letter, followed up seven days later with a phone call using a specific script with the goal of scheduling an appointment.

Software Requirements Checklist—Steps to Take

The above topics relate to the requirements you have when you automate your sales and marketing operations. Your responses determine the functional requirements the contact management software needs to satisfy in order to meet your business objectives. The steps you should take when determining what to automate include the following:

1. Evaluate the above topics in regard to your objectives. Your business circumstances may require additional topics be evaluated to properly define all the functional areas you need to computerize in order to maximize your ROI. Get input from as many people who will be working with the proposed system as possible and feasible.

2. Use the System Requirements Checklist that follows to define what you need your sales management system to handle. Check off the appropriate column based on the following criteria:

- Check the "Need" column if you must have the listed capability in your software. These items are essential to you in order to accomplish your critical objectives (as defined in question #1 of the management's and salespersons' perspective).

- Check the "Want" column if you would like, dependent on cost, the listed capability. The want column defines those items that are nice to have, but you could live without them if they cost too much.

- Leave blank any item that you do not need or want in the software.

3. Attach copies or samples of all required reports and forms you will need the system to produce.

Using this software requirements checklist approach provides you with the means of computing objectively the various software alternatives available for your specific business requirements and of selecting a solution that is the closest fit to your needs, based on your budget.

Fill out the following requirements form to help you determine the features you want in your sales management software system.

REQUIREMENTS FORM
DETERMINING WHAT TO AUTOMATE

1. List the specific objectives you have for automating; in other words, what do you hope to accomplish by automating?

    a. _____

    b. _____

    c. _____

    d _____

    e. _____

2. In order to accomplish the objectives in #1 above, who will need to share information and computer resources?

    _____

    _____

3. List the steps in your sales pipeline.

    a. _____

    b. _____

    c. _____

    d. _____

    e. _____

    f. _____

    g. _____

    h. _____

4. What critical information will you need to manage your sales pipeline?

    _____

    _____

5. **What critical reports do you need?**

   Presently receive:

   a. _____

   b. _____

   c. _____

   d. _____

   e. _____

   f. _____

   Would like, but presently don't get:

   a. _____

   b. _____

   c. _____

   d. _____

6. **Based on your previous responses, determine the critical data elements you need to keep track of.**

   Critical data elements:

   Always Need:

   Contact name, title, phone number, two address fields, city, state, zip code, secondary phone number (FAX).

   Highly Recommended:

   Progress level, lead source, business type, potential sale date, potential sale amount, interest, competitor.

7. **Do you need a contact management system that is linked with your present word processing software, or do you want the contact management software to provide the letter writing capabilities?**

   Need link with _____ word processing package.

8. **When you need to find information on a client or prospect, what are the indexes (or sorting criteria) will you need?**

   _____

   _____

9. **Do you want to produce quotes for clients and track their progress?**

   Yes _____   No _____

   If yes, you need order/quote integration.

10. **Do you want to integrate order processing and sales history information with your quote and contact management system (see year-to-date sales while talking to client on phone, update order processing system, etc.)?**

    Yes _____   No _____

    If yes, you need order processing integration, or use a windows-type program that will allow you to link multiple programs.

11. **Do you need the ability to create ad hoc reports on demand?**

    Yes _____   No _____

    If yes, you will require a report writer module.

12. **Do you want to track expenses for meals, mileage, etc.?**

    Yes _____   No _____

    If yes, you need expense-tracking capabilities in the software.

13. **Do you need the ability to read computerized databases of prospects, etc. into your system electronically?**

    Yes _____   No _____

    If yes, you need a data import capability to read the database into your sales management system. You must make certain the selected software can accommodate the type of data file you will need to import (ASCII, Dif, dBase, etc.).

14. **Do you need your system to check for duplicate records (to ensure the same prospect is not in the system twice)?**

    Yes _____   No _____

    If yes, what criteria do you want to check duplication on (e.g., main phone number)?

15. **What level of security will you need?**

    a. Simple password protection that allows access to a database

    b. More sophisticated user ratings that control what programs and files a user can access

16. **Do you need the ability to use "filters" and bring up to the screen only those records (prospects) that meet certain criteria?**

    Yes _____   No _____

    If yes, you need the software to allow you to select multiple fields in your database as filter centers (e.g., business type and zip code).

17. **Do you need to send faxes electronically?**

    Yes _____   No _____

    If yes, you need the software to handle this function and will need the software company to tell you which computer-based fax cards they work with.

18. **Do you want the computer to automatically dial the phone number of the person you are calling?**

    Yes _____   No _____

    If yes, you need the software to keep track of each contact's phone number and allow you to select the appropriate number to dial as well as allow you to connect the system to your phone line.

19. **Will you utilize telemarketers who will use interactive scripts with branching responses?**

    Yes _____   No _____

    If yes, you need a scripting module.

20. **Do you need two-way communications with your sales staff (send and receive information versus send only)?**

    Yes _____   No _____

    If yes, you need an import/export compatibility in the software. Software with direct line to remote users would be useful.

21. **Do you need to pre-define certain data input to ensure consistency throughout your system?**

    Yes _____   No _____

    If yes, you need the software to allow for pop-up windows with the ability to input what you want the selected items to be.

SYSTEM REQUIREMENTS LIST BY FUNCTIONAL AREA

I. Modules Available

User _____

	Need	Want	Comments
Contact management module (CMM)*			
— Low-end offering			
Windows version			
LAN version			
Telemarketing module with multiple branches			
Word processor—integrated with CMM above*			
— Automatic interface with popular w/p packages			
Distributed database— communications			
Report writer*			
Quotation/order processing integrated with CMM above			
Electronic mail			
Expense tracking			

* Highly recommended regardless of business

List Continues

SYSTEM REQUIREMENTS LIST BY FUNCTIONAL AREA
I. Modules Available (Continued)

User _____

	Need	Want	Comments
Market plan management			
Other			

SYSTEM REQUIREMENTS LIST BY FUNCTIONAL AREA

II. Systems Maintenance Functions

User _____

	Need	Want	Comments
Number of index fields — system set			
— User determined			
Security—password into program			
— Password and user rating File/field access			
Data importing/exporting capabilities — ASCII			
— Others required			
— Notes			
Keyboard macros			
Purging of history data options — By date			
— By account			
Duplicate record checking — Key index			
— Other required			
Data corruption housekeeping			
Pop up calculator			

List continues

SYSTEM REQUIREMENTS LIST BY FUNCTIONAL AREA

II. Systems Maintenance Functions (Continued)

User _____

	Need	Want	Comments
On-line help			
On-line systems information			
DOS hot key			
Print spooler			
Copy record function			
Send reports to screen			
—Disk			
Report — data dictionary			

SYSTEM REQUIREMENTS LIST BY FUNCTIONAL AREA

III. OTDB Profile

User _____

	Need	Want	Comments
Progress level/sales cycle			
— Required data field			
Sales projections			
— Sales rating			
— Potential sale			
— Target date			
— Product line			
Lead source			
Business type			
Salesperson/account executive			
Number of fields in record			
Number of user-defined fields			
Number of main contacts, name, title, phone			
Number of additional contacts, name, title, phone			
User-defined fields attributes			
— Character-based fields			
— Logical Yes or No fields			
— Date fields			

List continues

137

SYSTEM REQUIREMENTS LIST BY FUNCTIONAL AREA

III. OTDB Profile (Continued)

User _____

	Need	Want	Comments
— Dollar field with decimals			
— Required fields			
— Write to history			
— Hide/protect field attributes			
Report — OTDB profile			
— Sort by user-defined field			
— Contacts by progress level			
Projections report by date range			
— By salesperson			
Phone directory			

SYSTEM REQUIREMENTS LIST BY FUNCTIONAL AREA

IV. Agenda Management Functions

User _____

	Need	Want	Comments
Agenda by salesperson			
— Date conflict alarm			
— On-line daily to-do lists			
— Week at a glance			
— Month at a glance			
— Prioritized activities			
Pop-up calendar			
Recurring activities scheduled			
Ability to forward uncompleted items			
Automatic alarm of past-due "to-do's"			
Number of items scheduled per record			
Reports			
— Agenda by salesperson			
— To-do lists for user-selected period of time			

SYSTEM REQUIREMENTS LIST BY FUNCTIONAL AREA

V. Marketing Management Functions

User _____

	Need	Want	Comments
Activity tracking			
— Automatic update when recording activity calls, letters, tasks			
— User time & date stamp in history file			
— Objective & result per activity recorded in history file			
— User-defined activities written to history file			
Market plan management system			
— Number of steps in process			
— Automatic agenda activity creation			
— Report listing members			
— Merge with w/p			
— Progress level			
Sales forecasting by salesperson, company			
— By product line			
Bulk mailing			
— By selected criteria			

List continues

SYSTEM REQUIREMENTS LIST BY FUNCTIONAL AREA

V. Marketing Management Functions (Continued)

User _____

	Need	Want	Comments
Reports			
— Budget vs. actual			
— Proposals outstanding			

SYSTEM REQUIREMENTS LIST BY FUNCTIONAL AREA

VI. Data Management Functions

User _____

	Need	Want	Comments
Pop-up windows			
— User-defined windows with pre-defined input			
Required fields for data input — System set			
— User defined			
Inquiry filter by selected criteria			
Hot keys — menuing			
Free-form notes			
— Automatic date/user stamp			
— Key word lookup			
Length of call tracking			
Mass changes			

SYSTEM REQUIREMENTS LIST BY FUNCTIONAL AREA

VII. Communications Functions

User _____

	Need	Want	Comments
Remote update to central database—overwrite			
—Update if changed since last communication			
Direct link with remote users			
Hot Key interface to other programs			
Fax interface			
Automatic dial			

Chapter 9

HOW TO EVALUATE AND SELECT SALES MANAGEMENT SOFTWARE

Buying sales management software is much like buying anything else. You typically base your decision on the value your purchase will provide you versus the risk (cost, headaches, and probability of expectations being met) of the purchase. In the case of sales management software, there is an abundance of choices.

Hundreds of companies have developed packaged software for automating salespeople and sales management. The authors of these packages range from businesses operating out of basements to divisions of Fortune 1000 companies. In order to minimize your risk of automating your sales process, you need to understand the basic realities behind purchasing software.

Reality #1—There Are Limited Choices

Typically, you have three main choices when evaluating sales management software:

1. **Packaged software systems.** These systems do not allow you to modify or change the functionality of the software. Most of the low-cost packages fit into this category. Most of these packages allow you to change the names of some fields of information and use user-defined fields to "customize" what information you track. But you cannot change the way the software operates and often cannot change the way the screens look or operate. The benefit of these systems is typically their low cost. But you must be prepared to adapt your selling approach/process to the manner in which the package works.

2. **Modifiable packaged software.** These systems allow you or the author to modify or adapt the package to your specific needs. As in the case of the non-modifiable packages, these systems typically allow you to change the names of some fields and use user-defined fields. But in addition, you can customize or modify the functionality of these packages. Of course, whenever you begin modifying packaged software, be prepared to spend more money, and experience more headaches, than you originally expected. The companies that sell the ability to modify their software typically charge you for the "source code." The source code allows someone who knows how to program in the particular language the package is written in to make changes to the original package and write new programs that can be linked.

   If you decide you require software that you can modify, be aware of the following facts:

   • If you make changes to the package, any warranties are typically void. Understand how your vendor handles this situation.

- You may not be able to use any future upgrades, releases, or enhancements to the package. If you want to be in a position to use future releases, you must get the author of the software to guarantee future compatibility.

- You are always better off finding a package that will need no modifications to meet your critical requirements. If that is not possible, select the solution that will require the fewest changes unless special circumstances exist (e.g., a large discrepancy in cost between the package needing few changes and the one needing more).

3. **Custom programs**. These are software programs that are completely tailored to your exact needs. This approach will always cost more money, involve more grief to complete, and take longer than either of the two previous choices. The only reason to pursue this approach is if you cannot find a package that is close to your requirements, and the payback you will receive for successfully automating more than compensates for the costs. I suggest you use a powerful relational database program or fourth-generation language if you are going to customize your own system. If you do not know what a relational database or a fourth-generation language is, do not bother pursuing this approach unless you get professional assistance.

Reality #2—Perfect Solutions Do Not Exist

Focus your decision on meeting your critical requirements, but understand that the "perfect solution" does not exist. In over 14 years in the business, I have yet to find the perfect software system. Software programming is much more an art than a science. You should realize that you will have to make some compromises— and this is especially true when buying a computer system and automating your business. You will first have to determine how much you can afford to spend. You should base this decision on the payback you will receive from using the software effectively.

If you have a limited budget ($50–$300 for a single-user package), you probably will be forced to buy a nonmodifiable package that does not meet all your software requirements. If your budget is larger, your choices will be larger as well.

You will have to prioritize your software requirements so that you can better determine those areas where you cannot afford to trade off features and still accomplish your objectives. Your completed requirements checklist (Chapter 8) will help you define your needs.

Reality # 3—Know What You Want to Do

Automating inefficient manual systems will only speed up the mess; computers will not correct the inefficiencies. Prior to selecting a software package, clearly understand what you want to accomplish and develop the manual systems (people entering information, reports created for management review, and so forth) to support your objectives. Try to streamline your processes. Any activities that do not add value (e.g., help you sell more or make happy customers) should be eliminated prior to selecting or implementing your software system.

Reality # 4—Consultants or Sales Reps?

Many so-called "consultants" in the computer industry are nothing more than resellers of particular software who market themselves as "objective consultants." I am not suggesting that you should not do business with such consultants—only that you should be aware that they might steer you to buy products that they earn commissions on. In these situations, you need to make sure that the software will meet your business requirements and that the consultant can provide you with the assistance you will need to be productive using the software.

Reality # 5—Where to Get It

Sales management software is sold through several channels to the ultimate end user (yourself). The more expensive, modifiable software is usually sold by direct salespeople who work for the companies who wrote the package or "high-end" consulting firms who resell these packages and perform consulting services (programming, training, etc.) on an hourly basis to larger businesses. Firms with complex requirements or unique needs tend to purchase these more expensive systems (prices range from $5,000).

The lower-end, nonmodifiable software is typically sold by computer retail stores, discount stores, or through direct mail operations. These distribution channels will provide low costs but typically little support. If you buy from them, you will be pretty much on your own.

If you will need support to get the software installed and successfully implemented, a third channel is available. Many sales management software authors distribute their software through small reseller firms (called VARs in the computer industry), who earn a commission and provide many of the same services as the "high-end" consulting firms. VARs typically are smaller firms (1–16 people) that specialize in specific vertical markets or geographic areas. You can be referred to a VAR in your geographic area by contacting the software author and asking who supports their products in your area.

Reality # 6—Understand the Learning Curve and Support Requirements

Sales management software will not simply load into your computer and work. To become productive using the software, you will need to have access to people who either are experienced with the products you will be using or have the aptitude and time to learn on a trial-and-error basis. Understand what kind of support you will need prior to looking at software. Your support requirements will dictate which distribution channels you should use (for instance, VAR versus retail store).

Many of the software authors promote phone-based support of their products. If you do not have the expertise in-house, phone support is only marginally helpful. Many of the problems you may have will involve technical difficulties that will be difficult to solve over the phone or that will be caused by your hardware, operating system, or other software you may be running.

Keep these "realities" in your planning process as you prepare to purchase sales management software, so that your risk will be minimized.

How to Select a Software Vendor and Sales Management Package

Selecting a vendor and software product involves comparing the capabilities of the software product and vendor against the requirements necessary for you to meet your business objectives. The Requirements Checklist you filled out in Chapter 8 has been designed to help you determine the specific features and capabilities you need and to provide an easy means of performing this comparison.

If you are simply looking for a low-cost, low-end product, involving a cost of a few hundred dollars, the approach you should take is a lot less strenuous than if you are looking to automate your entire sales force or office, where you probably will need to invest thousands of dollars. The process I recommend for businesses to follow to select their software and vendor involves several steps:

1. **Have a clear picture of what you need to accomplish.** Fill out the Requirements Checklist in Chapter 8 per the instructions preceding it.

2. **Determine what type of support you will need from outside your firm.** Examples of support include the following:

   - Hardware purchase and installation—especially critical if you are implementing a LAN

   - Software installation and configuration on your hardware

   - Consulting assistance to determine how to pre-define your critical data elements, user-defined fields, sales pipeline levels, and such

   - On-site and/or classroom-based training on the selected software system

   - Operating systems training to handle data backup procedures, security, etc.

   - Ongoing "hand-holding" while you begin to use the software on an as-needed basis

   - Phone support to answer questions

   - Dial-in support via modem to diagnose and correct problems

   - Modifications to packaged software

3. **Locate packaged software alternatives that meet your needs.** I have included a list of some of the more popular sales management software packages for the IBM PC world in the Appendix. If you will need support, you can contact the authors of the software and ask them for local VARs of their product.

4. **Interview your list of potential vendors and compare their product to your Requirements Checklist.** Discuss with them what levels of support you think you will need. If you feel they could meet your needs, request that they prepare a preliminary proposal. A proposal should include the following:

- A copy of your Requirements Checklist filled out by them as to whether their product meets your requirements as-is.

- If the product does not meet your needs as-is, does the vendor have an alternate recommendation? What is the cost? For instance, if they sell a software product that is modifiable, what would it cost to make the required changes to meet your requirements?

- The costs of the software products they recommend to meet your Requirements Checklist.

- Warranty and support policies. Expected enhancements.

- Required hardware configuration and operating systems needed to run their software.

- Estimated support charges (hourly rates).

- At least three or four references.

- The approximate number of companies that are using this software.

- The number of employees who provide support and assistance.

- Sales brochures, sample reports, etc.

NOTE: Be prepared to answer questions from the vendors about your Requirements Checklist. If they are competent, they will want to clarify some of your requirements. If the vendor does not ask for clarification on some points, he or she may be interpreting your requirements to fit his or her needs, not yours.

After receiving this preliminary information, determine if the fit is close enough to your needs and if the estimated prices are within your budget. If the solution seems feasible, continue to the next step.

5. Schedule a detailed demonstration of their software. You want the vendor to show you how they will meet your requirements as described in your Requirements Checklist and discussions. I suggest you hold off seeing demonstrations until they have time to review your requirements so that they can be prepared to show you what you want to see. Go through your critical requirements in detail so that you can be certain the system will handle them adequately.

    If you like what you see in the demo, call their references and ask probing questions, such as these:

    *   Did the vendor meet their expectations on budget and on time ?

    *   What costs did they incur that were not originally planned?

    *   How often do they receive updates or enhancements on their software?

    *   How can you benefit from the references' experiences with the vendor?

6. Compare the finalists' offerings on an "apples-to-apples" basis. Determine which firm or firms will provide the most cost-justified solution to your needs. You will now be in a position to intelligently select a viable sales management software and vendor to purchase the products and services you will require to accomplish your objectives. In the Appendix, I have included a product evaluation criteria to assist you in evaluating software products and vendors.

    I highly recommend that you develop a contract with the selected vendor that spells out exactly what your expectations are, the cost of the products and services you will need, product warranties, and any commitments made to you by the vendor. Try to document all of your concerns so that, in the event of a problem or issue arising from the installation and implementation, the contract will spell out the remedies or obligations to resolve the matter quickly. It may be advisable for you to use an objective consultant experienced in these matters to assist in the selection and negotiation process to ensure that your interests are protected.

The Importance of Implementation Planning

If your business situation necessitates spending a considerable amount of money or involves major changes to the manner in which you do business, I highly recommend you develop a detailed implementation plan *prior* to beginning the installation process. An implementation plan is a document that spells out the exact steps required to implement the software in your business. It is a very detailed document that ultimately acts as a blueprint, outlining who will do what, when, and how.

The plan will need to be developed by you or a project manager on your staff and the selected vendor or consultants you are hiring to assist you. You should develop an implementation plan with the vendor. The vendor will need to spend a considerable amount of time and work through all the details of how you intend to use the system, in order to develop a useful plan. An implementation plan should include the following:

1. A work plan that lists, in chronological order, the sequence of events that need to occur. These events will detail what function needs to be completed (data entry, determination of pre-defined fields, training, etc.), who is responsible for performing this function (try to assign a specific person), and when the function will be completed (with a specific date).

2. An issues list with resolutions. In most cases, implementing a sales management system will necessitate changing something about how you presently operate. During the implementation planning process, you and the vendor

need to document any issues that will need to be resolved prior to using the software. Here are some examples of issues:

- Progress or sales cycle steps needing to be defined to manage the sales pipeline

- Any pre-defined data fields (such as lead sources) needing to be determined in order to ensure consistency and accuracy of your OTDB data

- Required changes to present management reporting processes or formats of reports

- Problems uncovered concerning people's job descriptions changing

- Data communication processes

- System security requirements

3. A training plan that determines who will be trained on what, when, and how. This is especially useful when you need to train salespeople and managers who operate out of multiple offices. In some cases, your vendor will train people you have assigned as "trainers" on how the software works. Your trainers will then be responsible for training the rest of your staff with the vendor available as backup. Other scenarios might include vendor training—either in a classroom or on a one-to-one basis.

4. A data-conversion plan listing what information you need to input into the computer system (or convert from an existing computer) and who will be responsible for managing this process. Data entry takes time, so make sure the people responsible have the time and resources (access to computer, information needing input available, etc.) to do the job. Your vendor should be very helpful in providing forms or assisting in these matters.

The money invested in implementation planning will be well spent because it will provide you with the following benefits:

1. A written plan outlining what you need to do to successfully implement your sales management system. This document will allow you to manage the installation process effectively.

2. An accurate budget detailing what it will cost you, in time and products, to become productive on your system. Upon completion of the implementation plan, a vendor should be able to provide firm pricing for each step of the plan, thereby minimizing surprises. Without a plan, you will discover that the issues and problems you encounter during implementation will cost you substantially more than originally expected. The implementation plan should become part of your contract.

3. The process of developing the implementation plan will educate you and your staff about what is involved in making the software work for your business. Remember, "an ounce of prevention is worth a pound of cure."

You should now have an understanding of what sales automation can mean for you and your business. You can now develop a Requirements Checklist and understand how to select the appropriate software system and vendor to meet your needs. Now you need to reflect on some of the pitfalls and problems to avoid when trying to use sales management software.

Chapter 10

WHAT NOT TO DO!

We have discussed how to use computers to supercharge your sales efforts. We have talked about what to look for in software, how to evaluate your needs, and so on. Learning what *not* to do can sometimes be as valuable as discovering what to do.

My years of experience working with automating various businesses has given me several valuable lessons learned from other companies' mistakes. The following is a summary of what *not to do* when automating your business:

1. **Don't buy anything until you know exactly what you are trying to accomplish.**

   If you do not have specific, measurable objectives for automating, I can guarantee you will fail. Computers are only tools; you must have specific objectives for how you plan on using the tool in order to buy one that has a good chance of doing the intended job. In other words, if you buy a hammer but need a screwdriver, you have a problem.

I have seen companies invest thousands of dollars in sales management software and training services only to show no productivity improvements after one or two years. In most cases, they had no clear objective as to what they needed to accomplish. As a result, they simply gave the software to their sales force and put a sales administrator in charge of the project. The poor administrator had no real idea as to what they wanted to accomplish and had no authority to get the sales managers and sales staff to use the system. The net result was that nothing was gained for either the sales team or the company.

2. **Don't buy without an objective comparison.**

Subjective feelings can influence your buying decisions. It is important to have an objective method of comparing alternatives that goes beyond your liking the color, the salesperson, the speed, and so on. The fact that you bought your software from a "nice guy" becomes irrelevant when you have problems getting the system to work properly in your business situation.

One of the major advantages of the Requirements Checklist (Chapter 8) is that it provides you with an objective means of evaluating the software that goes beyond your subjective feelings. Use it.

3. **Don't generalize your software requirements.**

One very common mistake that people make when evaluating software is to oversimplify or generalize their system requirements.

One example of generalizing your requirements would be to assume that because one software alternative allows you to create as many user-defined fields as you want, that you can somehow get it to handle management of your sales pipeline. You assume that if you categorize one user-defined field as a "sales cycle" field you will be able to generate reports that sort number of contacts by sales step.

The fact is, most salespeople will not bother updating a "sales cycle" field upon completion of a call or meeting. You will need the system to require automatically, upon completion of the call/meeting, etc., an update of the sales cycle field, or the information will probably be inaccurate. Most software, in their user-defined fields, do not offer this capability. Also, to create meaningful reports, you need the software to easily allow you to sort your sales steps in a logical order. Some *ad hoc* reporting systems do not enable you to control easily the order in which your report sequences the information.

4. **Don't believe what you don't see.**

It is very common during product demonstrations for a computer salesperson to tell you that a critical feature you require is handled in their software. It is one thing to hear it, but you must see it work in the way you need it, to be certain your requirements will be effectively met. This is especially true for calendar and activity-tracking functions. The software must be easy to use for salespeople to get up to speed and be more productive.

5. **Don't assume—ask questions.**

Leave no loose ends. If you assume, for instance, that the warranty on your hardware and software means that when you have a problem, your vendor will come on-site and fix it at no cost, you may be surprised. Many warranties require your shipping the product back to the manufacturer, who will repair the problem and ship the goods back (especially true for hardware). If someone needs to be on-site to correct your problem, you will be charged for their time.

Don't assume that you understand how you will be supported by the vendor you buy your products from. What are the ongoing costs? If your business grows, can the system expand with it? What will your expansion costs be? The "fine print" that you assumed was in your favor will usually come back and haunt you.

One of the major benefits of developing a software Implementation plan is that is forces you to look at your assumptions and understand the ramifications on you and your business. The logistical assumptions some businesses make about what is involved in installing software and loading critical information can come as quite a suprise during "the moment of truth": that moment when you realize the assumptions you made were incorrect. Your new software does not seem to work correctly and you do not have all the information you need to get started. These experiences tend to cause your staff's morale to hit the floor at the same time your budget goes through the ceiling.

6. **Don't buy solely based on the price:**

The cheapest system may not be the most cost-effective for your business requirements. Typically, the cost of the software and hardware products are only a small part of the total cost to get the software and hardware installed and effectively used by your people. Look at the big picture. Money wisely spent up front can translate into major savings later.

You will be better off buying a product that meets your critical needs and comes with the support services you will need to make it work, even if it is more expensive than a product that costs less but does not satisfy your critical needs and has insufficient support backup. Remember: you are investing in a sales management system not to spend as little as possible but to get as high a return as possible.

Base your budget on what your payback will be upon successful implementation of a solution that helps you meet your sales objectives.

7. **Don't underestimate the effort required to automate your sales management system.**

   Computers do not plug in the wall, boot up, and work. It takes a great deal of thought and effort to analyze how you want them to work and to use them effectively. You must make the time available to the people responsible to properly install the system, load your data, be trained, and actually use the system for a number of weeks before final implementation.

   Salespeople tend to be resistant to change if they do not see how the change will benefit them. Automating the sales process will necessitate that the salespeople change the way they work. They will need to use the software for managing sales activities, and to write letters, notes, and management reports.

8. **Don't drop the project on someone's lap.**

   Do not buy a computer system without involving, to some degree, those people who will be responsible for using and manging the computer system. This is critical when dealing with salespeople. They must see how the new system is going to help them make more money and make their lives easier, or they will not use it. You would be surprised at how creative people can be when they want to sabotage something they feel threatened by.

   One of the most typical mistakes I have seen businesses make is lack of effective project management. What I mean by project management is having someone on your staff who is not only responsible for seeing the project through to its successful completion, but has the time, authority (either direct or through management), and experience to do the job. Putting an inexperienced person who has little time and no authority in charge of a project will guarantee total failure.

Remember: if something sounds too good to be true, it usually is. Computer systems can be invaluable tools for your business, but you need realistic expectations and the appropriate tools to get your job done.

Chapter 11

CONCLUSIONS

Supercharging your sales efforts involves using computer hardware and software as tools to maximize your productivity, provide timely and accurate analysis of your selling activities, and give you access to the information you need to sell smart.

As with any tool, in order to select the best software to automate your sales team, the first step you must take is to determine what you plan to accomplish using it. The process of determining how the tool will help you accomplish your objectives lays the groundwork for selecting the appropriate tool to get the job completed efficiently.

Achieve the Benefits of Supercharging Your Sales Process

The advantages of managing your Opportunities To Do Business as assets of your business are tremendous. The sales pipeline will provide you the framework within which you can manage your OTDB database and reap great rewards.

Setting specific, measurable goals and using the computer to track your results will keep you on target and minimize the "feast or famine" cycles so common in today's selling environments.

Utilizing the follow-up and agenda management capabilities of contact management software will ensure that you do not drop any balls and will minimize missed opportunities. Customer service will also improve by using this tool to keep in contact with clients and to follow up on their satisfaction with your products/services.

Management can also use computers to enhance communication, marketing effectiveness, and overall productivity, while improving the control and continuity of their OTDB assets.

Ingredients of Success

The ingredients of successful sales automation include the following:

- **Think Big but Start Small.** Have a clear picture of what you want the end results to be. Thinking big involves "stretching" yourself and your firm by aiming at high targets. Starting small means breaking your system's installation into "bite-sized" pieces or steps. For instance, pilot the software project with a few motivated salespeople to work the kinks out before attempting to automate your entire office. Approach the implementation process on a gradient basis—one step at a time. Determine the steps you need to take in order to accomplish your big picture, while focusing on the immediate steps at hand.

- **Discipline = Success.** The most critical ingredient to success is discipline and "stick-to-it-ness." I can guarantee that if you use the appropriate tool on a daily basis, you will achieve phenomenal results. I can also guarantee that during the course of your installation, problems will arise. I have never seen a computer system implemented without unexpected circumstances and problems. Work your way through these difficulties.

- **If you do not have the expertise, seek help.** Computer software and hardware can be complicated things to figure out how to get to work properly. Someone needs to understand the technical jargon and issues in order to set up the software and hardware components. If you do not have this expertise in-house (either yourself, an employee, or friend), hire someone who does (e.g., consultant, VAR). If you are planning to use only a single-user system (stand-alone PC), your needs are much simpler. But, if you have the need for multi-user systems (Local Area Network with several people working at the same time) or complicated communications (several remote users and/or offices), you *require* someone who has successfully done these things before.

I have explained what to automate and how to evaluate and select sales management software in previous chapters of this book. This information will provide you with an excellent framework to develop your own Software Requirements Checklist and select an appropriate software product to meet your needs.

If your business requirements go beyond what you feel your expertise can handle, I strongly suggest you hire an objective consultant who has the appropriate experience and credentials to assist you in this important process. It is an excellent idea for you to fill out the Software Requirements Checklist in any case, because it will help you organize your thoughts and assist any outside professional.

My original reason for writing this book was to provide a concise, down-to earth, non-computerese description of how to automate salespeople successfully. I sincerely hope I have accomplished my objective and that you will reap the rewards and accomplishments you desire.

If I can be of any assistance, please contact me at my office:

Jon C. Liberman
Checkers, Simon & Rosner
One South Wacker Drive—17th Floor
Chicago, Illinois 60606
(312) 917-0685

APPENDIX

Product Evaluation Methodology

I have evaluated the ten products compared in the *Systems Requirements List—Product Comparisons* by a combination of phone interviews with the manufacturer of the software, self-running demos, and, in some cases, product demonstrations by VARs or representatives of the products. The purpose of this evaluation is to provide you with an overview of what the products functionally can accommodate. You must evaluate the software yourself to determine how well it will fit your unique requirements. Use the product comparison matrix as a means of narrowing down the list to those two to four systems that best meet your software requirements and budget and perform your detailed investigation on those. You can also request any vendor who is not evaluated or who has an updated version to respond to your requirements checklist and thereby compare them objectively.

Remember that software products are usually being updated and changed on a regular basis. As a result, new versions of the evaluated software will probably have different capabilities and costs. The vendor evaluation may become dated information. The information provided by the vendors, such as number of installations, employees, technical employees, etc., has not been verified.

Although all the vendors provide some means of phone support, my experience is that it typically will take you several calls to actually get through to a person who can answer your questions. The phone-tag and voice mail maze of tracking down a human being can be quite frustrating.

Hundreds of companies have written sales management and contact management software. Each software system has unique qualities and often categorizes the same function with different labels. There are also various ways in which the software is "packaged" for resale.

Some firms have "low-end" offerings that provide just about the same functionality as their high-end product, only with limits as to the number of records the low-end product can handle (e.g., 300 prospects is the limit; over 300 you have to upgrade to the high-end product, etc.).

To assist you in understanding how I have organized the system requirements list by functional area checklist, review the following:

1. Modules Available:

   Lists the software modules you may need in your contact management software to meet your needs. The contact management module typically handles all the items with a Y entry. If the module requires the purchase of additional software to handle the listed capabilities, it is noted with a 3P (third-party product) in the checklist or has an * and is explained in the notes at the end of the requirements checklist.

2. System Maintenance Functions:

   Lists the system-wide capabilities you need the software to handle. In other words, the "housekeeping" functions you need the system to perform.

3. OTDB Profile:

Lists the data elements the software captures. Includes the user-defined fields and the user-defined fields attributes. (Attributes are the options a user has in terms of defining the type of information that the field can contain—such as a date field (12/21/93); dollar field with decimals ($1,200.45); logical field (Y)es or (N)o; required field—meaning when the cursor is on the field the user must input data; write-to-history field which automatically updates the history file whenever the field is updated).

4. Agenda Management Profile:

   Lists the agenda and calendar-related capabilities needed in the software.

5. Marketing Management Function:

   Lists the activity-reporting capabilities and marketing plan capabilities of the software.

6. Data Management Function:

   Lists the data manipulation and inquiry capabilities of the software.

7. Communications Functions:

   Lists the data communication capabilities of the system.

Product Evaluation Criteria

ACT for Windows

Company Name: **Contact Software International, Inc.**

Telephone No. **800-365-0606**

Contact: **Sales**

Address: **1625 W. Crosby Rd., Suite 132
Carrollton, TX 75006**

Product name: **ACT for Windows**   Version: **1.202**

Years in business: No. of revisions since inception:

No. of installations: **350,000 +**   No. of employees: **100 +**

No. of technical employees: **N/A**

Distribution channels: **Direct Sales, VARs, Retail, Distribution**

Support policy: **Free phone support**

Documentation available: user manual, tutorial

Operating systems supported:: **Windows**

Language written in: **MAC, C**

Source code available: **No**

Pricing:

DOS/MAC	$ 395	Merge/convert utility **	$ 295
Windows	$ 495		
1st Act—DOS *	$ 79.95		
LAN—1–2 users	$ 595		
LAN—3–5 users	$1,295		
—Each add'l user	$ 395		

*   Only one database and fewer features
** Takes data from other packages and merges into ACT

All pricing and revision information subject to change

ACT for DOS

Company Name: **Contact Software International, Inc.**

Telephone No.   **800-365-0606**

Contact: **Sales**

Address: **1625 W. Crosby Rd., Suite 132
Carrollton, TX 75006**

Product name: **ACT for DOS**   Version: **2.11A**

Years in business: No. of revisions since inception:

No. of installations: **350,000 +**   No. of employees: **100 +**

No. of technical employees: **N/A**

Distribution channels: **Direct Sales, VARs, Retail, Distribution**

Support policy: **Free phone support**

Documentation available: user manual, tutorial

Operating systems supported::   **DOS, Novell**

Language written in: **C++**

Source code available: **No**

Pricing:

DOS/MAC	$ 395	Merge/convert utility **	$ 295
Windows	$ 495		
1st Act—DOS *	$ 79.95		
LAN—1–2 users	$ 595		
LAN—3–5 users	$1,295		
—Each add'l user	$ 395		

*   Only one database and fewer features
**   Takes data from other packages and merges into ACT

All pricing and revision information subject to change

BIZ BASE GOLD

Company Name: **CReagh Computer Systems**

Telephone No. **800-833-8892**

Contact: **Sales**

Address: **16855 W. Bernardo Dr., Suite 201**
San Diego, CA 92127-1627

Product name: **BIZ BASE GOLD**   Version: **3.0**

Years in business: 4   No. of revisions since inception: 6

No. of installations: **30,000 +**   No. of employees: **16**

No. of technical employees: **4**

Distribution channels: **Direct Sales, VARs, Distribution**

Support policy: **Unlimited phone support ***

Documentation available: **Full reference manual**

Operating systems supported:: **DOS, Windows, Novell**

Language written in: **Compiled Clipper, C and Assembler**

Source code available: **No**

Pricing:

DOS/Windows $ 295

LAN **—1–4 users $ 695

LAN—5–8 users $ 995

— Unlimited $1,395

*   As long as you are using current version. Each upgrade has a charge. Call for details.

**   Windows version not available on LAN

All pricing and revision information subject to change

EMIS II

Company Name: **EMIS Software**

Telephone No. **800-593-8499**

Contact: **Sales**

Address: **901 North East Loop 410, Suite 526**
San Antonio, TX 78209

Product name: **EMIS II**   Version: **3.02**

Years in business: **6**   No. of revisions since inception:—9

No. of installations: **3,500 +**   No. of employees: **14**

No. of technical employees: **6**

Distribution channels: **Direct Sales, VARs ***

Support policy: **30 day phone support ****

Documentation available: **Tutorial; reference user manual**

Operating systems supported: **DOS, Novell**

Language written in: **Basic, C, Assembler**

Source code available: **Yes; call for details**

Pricing:

EMIS I—DOS***	$ 695
EMIS II—DOS	$1,995
LAN—per user	$ 695
Word Perfect 5.1 interface, per user	$ 100

*   The VAR who assisted me—David James and Associates, David Hubanks, 312-258-1414.
** Support contract available; call for details.
*** Same functions as II, but only one database and no report writer.

All pricing and revision information subject to change

GOLDMINE

Company Name: **ELAN Software Corp.**

Telephone No. **800-654-3526**

Contact: **Natalie Burdick or Brenda Christensen**

Address: **17383 Sunset Blvd., Suite 101
Pacific Palisades, CA 90272**

Product name: **GoldMine**   Version: **25**

Years in business: **4**   No. of revisions since inception: **3**

No. of installations: **12,000 +**   No. of employees: **30**

No. of technical employees: **7**

Distribution channels: **Direct Sales, VARs, Distribution**

Support policy: **Unlimited phone support ***

Documentation available: **User manual**

Operating systems supported: **DOS, Novell, Unix**

Language written in: **Clipper**

Source code available: **No**

Pricing:

DOS	$ 295
LAN 1–5 users	$ 895
—6–10 users	$1,495
—11–25 users	$2,995
—Over 25 users	Call for price
Zipcode Database	$ 79.95

*   As long as you are using current or one previous version.

All pricing and revision information subject to change

MARKET FORCE +

Company Name: **Software of the Future**

Telephone No. **800-766-7355**

Contact: **Sales**

Address: **P.O. Box 531650**
Grand Prairie, TX 75053

Product name: **MarketForce +** Version: **5.54**

Years in business: **8** No. of revisions since inception: **5**

No. of installations: **20,000 +** No. of employees: **30**

No. of technical employees: **10**

Distribution channels: **Direct Sales, VARs *, Distribution in Europe**

Support policy: **30 day phone support no charge ****

Documentation available: **Reference manual, Getting Started manual,**
Installation Guide

Operating systems supported: **DOS, Novell**

Language written in: **Btrieve and Assembler**

Source code available: **No**

Pricing:

DOS	$ 695	Duplicate finder utility	$ 249
LAN 1–5 users	$2,495	File conversion	$ 249
Ea. add'l user	$ 995	Distributed database—	
Corporate system—		LAN server	$2,995
1st 10 users	$1,500	Remote LAN	$ 995
Ea. add'l user	$1,000	Ea. remote user	$ 299
Advanced report writer	$2,995	Host program interface	$ 995

* VAR who assisted me—Technol Corp., Deepak Mansukhani, 800-735-7355
** Fee for additional support. Call for details.

All pricing and revision information subject to change.

PACKRAT for Windows

Company Name: **Polaris Software**

Telephone No. **800-722-5728**

Contact: **Sales**

Address: **17150 Via Del Campo, Suite 307**
San Diego, CA 92127

Product name: **PackRat for Windows**   Version: **5.0**

Years in business: **6**   No. of revisions since inception: **5**

No. of installations: **N/A**   No. of employees: **N/A**

No. of technical employees: **N/A**

Distribution channels: **Direct Sales, VARs, Retail, Distribution, Catalog**

Support policy: **Unlimited phone support to registered users ***

Documentation available: **Getting Started manual, Reference Guide,**
PackRat BASIC manual

Operating systems supported: **Windows; Novell 4th Qtr. '93**

Language written in: **C**

Source code available: **No ****

Pricing:

Windows	$395
Novell—1–3 users	$695
—Each add'l user	$150

*   Current & one previous version
** A PackRat Basic language is available for programmers to modify the program.

All pricing and revision information subject to change

SNAP for Windows

Company Name: **Sales Technologies**

Telephone No. **404-841-4000**

Contact: **Sales**

Address: **3399 Peachtree Rd. N.E., Lenox Bld. Suite 700
Atlanta, GA 30326**

Product name: **SNAP for Windows**   Version: **1.2**

Years in business: **11**   No. of revisions since inception: **7**

No. of installations: **40,000 +**   No. of employees: **500**

No. of technical employees: **300**

Distribution channels: **Direct Sales**

Support policy: **Support contract available—call for details**

Documentation available: User release manual, server manual,
configuration manual

Operating systems supported: **Windows, Novell, Unix, OS/2 on server**

Language written in: **C++**

Source code available: **No**

Pricing:

Windows–P	$1,195	Configuration tool kit	
Novell–server	$3,000	for Windows—	
—Each add'l user	$ 995	1–200 users	$20,000
OS/2–server	$4,000	DOS—single user	$ 895
Unix–server	$4,000		

All pricing and revision information subject to change

TELEMAGIC

Company Name: **Remote Control International**

Telephone No. **800-835-MAGIC**

Contact: **Sales**

Address: **5928 Pascal Court**
Carlsbad, CA 92008

Product name: **Telemagic** Version: **12.3F**

Years in business: **8** No. of revisions since inception: **7**

No. of installations: **250,000 +** No. of employees: **60**

No. of technical employees: **12**

Distribution channels: **VARs ***

Support policy: **90 days free phone support ****

Documentation available: **Welcome guide, Getting Started, full reference manual**

Operating systems supported: **DOS, MAC, Novell, Unix, AS/400 through 3rd party**

Language written in: **Clipper**

Source code available: **Yes; cost $4,995**

Pricing:

DOS	$ 495	Unix–unlimited	$2,695
LAN 1–3 users	$1,295	AS/400	Call for price
—4–10 users	$1,995		
—11–20 users	$2,695		
—21–50 users	$3,995		
—Unlimited users	$9,995		

* VAR who assisted me—Accessem Inc., Ronen Ben–Dror, 312-264-4770.
** Extended support available for a fee

All pricing and revision information subject to change

TOTALL MANAGER

Company Name: **Automation Technologies Inc.**

Telephone No. **800-777-6368**

Contact: **Joseph Pettit**

Address: **2563 East Willow Hills Dr.**
Sandy, UT 84093

Product name: **Total Manager**   Version: **3.0**

Years in business: **8**   No. of revisions since inception: **8**

No. of installations: **12,000 +**   No. of employees: **12**

No. of technical employees: **4**

Distribution channels: **Direct Sales, VARs, Retail**

Support policy: **90 days free phone support; fee after; call for details**

Documentation available: **User manual**

Operating systems supported: **DOS, Windows, Novell**

Language written in: **FoxBase**

Source code available: **No**

Pricing:

TM DOS/Windows	$ 495
LAN—5 users	$1,495
—over 5 users	Call for price

All pricing and revision information subject to change

Systems Requirements List—Product Comparisons

Legend

Y=System handles function
N=System does not handle function
3P=System handles function only with third party
products that must be purchased separately
YW=System handles function only with Windows version
UL=Unlimited number
UD=User defined fields
RW=Report writer needed
( )=Notes—See attached notes for that vendor

I. Modules Available

	Software Package									
	ACT 2.11A	ACT for Windows	BIZ BASE 3.0	EMIS II 3.0	GOLD MINE 3.0	MARKET FORCE+ 5.0	PACK RAT—Windows	SNAP—windows	TELEMAGIC 3.0	TOTAL MANAGER 3.0
Contact Management Module (CMM)*	Y	Y	Y	Y	Y	Y	Y	Y	Y	Y
— Low End offering	N	N	Y	Y	N	N	N	Y	N	N
Windows version	N	Y	Y	N	N	N	Y	Y	Y	Y
LAN version	Y	Y	Y	Y	Y	Y	N(1)	Y	Y	Y
Telemarketing Module with multiple branches	N	N	N	N	Y	Y	N	N	3P	N
Wordprocessor—integrated with CMM above*	Y	Y	Y	Y	Y(1)	Y	N	N	Y	Y
— Automatic interface with popular WP packages	N	N	Y	Y(1)	Y	N	Y	Y	Y(1)	Y(1)
Distributed Database— Communications	Y	Y	Y	Y	Y	Y	Y	3P	3P	Y
Report Writer*	Y	Y	Y	Y	Y	Y	Y	Y	Y	3P
Quotation/Orderprocessing integrated with CMM above	N	N	Y	N	N	N(1)	N	3P	N(2)	N
Electronic Mail	N	N	Y(1)	N	Y	N	Y	3P	Y(3)	N
Expense Tracking	Y	N	Y	N	N	Y	Y(2)	N	3P	Y
Market Plan Management	N	N	N	N	N	N(2)	N	Y	N	Y

I. Modules Available (Continued)

	Software Package									
	ACT 2.11A	ACT for Windows	BIZ BASE 3.0	EMIS II 3.0	GOLD MINE 3.0	MARKET FORCE+ 5.0	PACK RAT—Windows	SNAP—windows	TELEMAGIC 3.0	TOTAL MANAGER 3.0
Other	Y	Y	N	Y(2)	Y(2)	Y	Y(3)	Y(1)	Y	N

*Highly recommended regardless of business

II. Systems Maintenance Functions

	Software Package									
	ACT 2.11A	ACT for Windows	BIZ BASE 3.0	EMIS II 3.0	GOLD MINE 3.0	MARKET FORCE+ 5.0	PACK RAT—Windows	SNAP—windows	TELEMAGIC 3.0	TOTAL MANAGER 3.0
Number of index fields — system set	7	7	5	8	15	6	UL	2	3	6
— User determined	0	0	5	0	5	3	UL	UL	7	91
Security—Password into program	Y	Y	Y	Y	Y	N(3)	Y	Y	Y	Y
— Password and User rating — File/Field access	N	N	N	Y	Y	N(3)	Y	Y	Y	Y
Data Importing/Exporting capabilities — ASCII	Y	Y	Y	Y	Y	Y	Y	Y	Y	Y
— Others Required	Y	Y	Y	N	Y	Y(4)	Y	N	Y	Y
— Notes	Y	Y	Y	Y	Y	N	Y	Y	Y	Y
Keyboard macros	Y	Y	Y	Y	Y	Y	Y	N	Y	N
Purging of history data options — By date	Y	Y	N	Y	Y	Y	Y	Y	Y	Y
— By account	Y	Y	Y	Y	Y	Y	Y	Y	Y	Y
— Notes	Y	Y	Y	Y	Y	Y	Y	Y	3P	Y
Duplicate record checking — Key Index	N	N	Y	N	Y	Y	Y	Y	Y	Y
— Other required	N	N	N	N	N	N	N	Y	3P	N
Data corruption housekeeping	Y	Y	Y	Y	Y	Y	Y	Y	Y	Y

II. Systems Maintenance Functions (Continued)

	Software Package									
	ACT 2.11A	ACT for Windows	BIZ BASE 3.0	EMIS II 3.0	GOLD MINE 3.0	MARKET FORCE+ 5.0	PACK RAT—Windows	SNAP—windows	TELEMAGIC 3.0	TOTAL MANAGER 3.0
Pop up Calculator	Y	Y	Y	N	Y	Y	N	Y	Y	Y
On-line help	Y	Y	Y	Y	Y	Y	Y	Y	Y	Y
On-line systems information	Y	Y	Y	Y	Y	N	Y	Y	Y	Y
DOS Hot Key	Y	YW	Y	Y	Y	Y	YW	YW	Y	Y
Print spooler	N	N	N	N	Y	Y	N	N	N	Y
Copy record function	Y	Y	Y	Y	Y	Y	Y	Y	Y	Y
Send reports to screen	Y	Y	Y	Y	Y	Y	Y	Y	Y	Y
—Disk	Y	Y	Y	Y	Y	Y	N	Y	Y	Y
Report — Data dictionary	N	N	N(2)	N	N	Y	N	RW	RW	Y

III. OTDB Profile

	Software Package									
	ACT 2.11A	ACT for Windows	BIZ BASE 3.0	EMIS II 3.0	GOLD MINE 3.0	MARKET FORCE+ 5.0	PACK RAT—Windows	SNAP—windows	TELEMAGIC 3.0	TOTAL MANAGER 3.0
Progress Level/Sales Cycle	N	N	N	Y	N	N	N	Y	N	Y
— Required data field	N	N	N	Y	N	N	N	Y	N	Y
Sales Projections	RW	RW	Y(3)	RW	Y	RW	RW	Y	RW	RW
— Sales Rating	UD	UD	Y	UD	Y	UD	UD	Y	UD	UD
— Potential Sale	UD	UD	Y	UD	Y	UD	UD	Y	UD	UD
— Target Date	UD	UD	Y	UD	Y	UD	UD	Y	UD	UD
— Product line	UD	UD	Y	UD	Y	UD	UD	Y	UD	UD
Lead source	Y	Y	UD	UD	Y	Y	UD	Y	UD	Y
Business type	UD	UD	UD	UD	UD	Y	UD	Y	UD	Y
Salesperson/Account Executive	UD	UD	UD	UD	UD	UD	UD	Y	UD	Y
Number of fields in record	45	45	90	18	22	97	UL	200	16	97
Number of user-defined fields	29	70	50	UL	UL	27	UL	UL (4)	250 (4)	64
Number of main contacts, name, title, phone	1	1	1	1	1	2	1	UL (3)	1	1
Number of additional contacts, name, title, phone	2	2	UL (4)	UL (3)	UL	UL	UL	UL	UD (5)	2

III.   OTDB Profile (Continued)

	Software Package									
	ACT 2.11A	ACT for Windows	BIZ BASE 3.0	EMIS II 3.0	GOLD MINE 3.0	MARKET FORCE+ 5.0	PACK RAT—Windows	SNAP—windows	TELEMAGIC 3.0	TOTAL MANAGER 3.0
User-defined fields										
— Character-based fields	Y	Y	Y	Y	Y	Y	Y	Y	Y	Y
— Logical Yes or No fields	N	N	Y	Y	N	Y	Y	Y	N	Y
— Date fields	N	Y	Y	Y	Y	Y	Y	Y	Y	Y
— Dollar field with decimals	Y	Y	Y	Y	Y	Y	Y	Y	Y	Y
— Required fields	N	N	N	Y	Y	Y	Y	Y	Y	Y
— Write to history	Y	Y	N	Y	N	N	N	Y	N	Y
— Hide/protect field attributes	Y	Y	N	N	Y	N	Y	Y	N	Y
Report — OTDB profile	N	N	Y	RW	N	Y	RW	Y	Y	Y
— Sort by user-defined field	N	N	RW	Y	Y	RW	RW	RW	Y	RW
— Contacts by progress level	N	N	N	Y	N	N	N	RW	N	Y
Projections report by date range	RW	RW	Y	RW	Y	Y	RW	Y	RW	RW
— by salesperson	RW	RW	Y	RW	Y	Y	RW	Y	RW	RW
Phone directory	Y	Y	Y	Y	Y	Y	Y	RW	Y	Y

IV. Agenda Management Profile

	Software Package									
	ACT 2.11A	ACT for Windows	BIZ BASE 3.0	EMIS II 3.0	GOLD MINE 3.0	MARKET FORCE+ 5.0	PACK RAT—Windows	SNAP—windows	TELEMAGIC 3.0	TOTAL MANAGER 3.0
Agenda by salesperson	Y	Y	Y	Y	Y	Y(5)	N(4)	Y	Y(6)	Y
— Date conflict alarm	Y	Y	Y	Y	Y	Y	Y	Y	N	Y
— On-line daily to-do lists	Y	Y	Y	N(4)	Y	Y(5)	Y	Y	Y	Y
— Week at a glance	Y	Y	Y	Y	Y	Y	Y	Y	Y	Y
— Month at a glance	Y	Y	Y	Y	Y	Y	Y	Y	Y	Y
— Prioritized activities	Y	Y	N	N	Y	N	Y	Y	N	Y
Pop-up calendar	Y	Y	Y	Y	Y	Y	Y	Y	Y(6)	Y
Recurring activities scheduled	N	Y	Y	N	Y	Y	Y	Y	Y(6)	Y
Ability to forward uncompleted items	N(1)	N(1)	Y	Y	Y	Y	Y	Y	Y	Y
Automatic alarm of past-due "to-do's"	Y	Y	Y	N	Y	N	Y	N(4)	Y	Y
Number of items scheduled per record	UL	UL	UL	1(5)	UL	UL	UL	UL	1	UL
Reports										
— Agenda by salesperson	Y	Y	RW	Y	Y	Y	Y	Y	Y	Y
— To-do lists for user-selected period of time	Y	Y	RW	N	Y	Y	Y	Y	Y(6)	Y

V. Marketing Management Function

	Software Package									
	ACT 2.11A	ACT for Windows	BIZ BASE 3.0	EMIS II 3.0	GOLD MINE 3.0	MARKET FORCE+ 5.0	PACK RAT—Windows	SNAP—windows	TELEMAGIC 3.0	TOTAL MANAGER 3.0
Activity tracking	Y	Y	Y	Y	Y	Y	Y	Y	Y(7)	Y
— Automatic update when recording activity calls, letters, tasks	Y	Y	Y	Y	Y	Y	Y(5)	Y	N(7)	Y
— User time & date stamp in history file	Y	Y	Y	N	Y	Y	Y	Y	Y	Y
— Objective & result per activity recorded in history file	N	N	Y	Y	Y	Y	Y	Y	Y	Y
— User-defined activities written to history file	Y	Y	N	N	N	N	N	Y	N	Y
Market plan management system	N	N	N	N	N	Y(2)	N	Y	Y(8)	Y
— Number of steps in process	N	N	N	N	N	UL	N	UL	1	UL
— Automatic agenda activity creation	N	N	Y	N	Y	Y(2)	N	Y	N	Y
— Report listing members	N	N	Y	N	Y	Y(2)	N	Y	RW	Y
— Merge with WP	N	N	Y	Y	Y	Y(2)	Y	Y	Y	Y
— Progress level	N	N	N	N	N	N	N	Y	N	Y
Sales forecasting by salesperson, company	RW	RW	Y(3)	RW	Y	Y	RW	Y	RW	RW
— By product line	UD	UD	Y(3)	UD	Y	UD	UD	Y	UD	UD
Bulk mailing	Y	Y	Y	Y	Y	Y	Y	Y	Y	Y
— By selected criteria	Y	Y	Y	Y	Y	Y	Y	Y	Y	Y

V. Marketing Management Function (Continued)

	Software Package									
	ACT 2.11A	ACT for Windows	BIZ BASE 3.0	EMIS II 3.0	GOLD MINE 3.0	MARKET FORCE+ 5.0	PACK RAT—Windows	SNAP—windows	TELEMAGIC 3.0	TOTAL MANAGER 3.0
Reports										
— Budget vs. actual	N	N	N	N	N	Y(2)	N	N	N	N
— Proposals outstanding	RW	RW	Y(3)	Y	Y	RW	RW	Y	RW	RW

VI. Data Management Function

	Software Package									
	ACT 2.11A	ACT for Windows	BIZ BASE 3.0	EMIS II 3.0	GOLD MINE 3.0	MARKET FORCE+ 5.0	PACK RAT—Windows	SNAP—windows	TELEMAGIC 3.0	TOTAL MANAGER 3.0
Pop-up window	Y	Y	Y	Y	Y	Y	Y	Y	Y	Y
— User-defined windows with pre-defined input	Y	Y	Y	Y	Y	Y	Y	Y	N	Y
Required fields for data input — System set	N	N	N	N	Y	N	Y	N	Y	Y
— User defined	N	N	N	Y	Y	Y	Y	N	N	Y
Inquiry filter by selected criteria	Y	Y	Y	Y	Y	Y	Y	Y	Y	Y
Hot keys — menuing	Y	Y	Y	Y	N	Y	Y	Y	Y	Y
Free-form notes	Y	Y	Y	Y	Y	Y	Y	Y	Y	Y
— Automatic date/user stamp	Y	Y	Y	Y	Y	Y	N	N	Y	Y
—Key word lookup	Y	Y	Y	N	Y	Y	Y	Y	Y	N
Length of call tracking	Y	Y	Y	N	Y	Y	Y	N(5)	Y	Y
Mass changes	N(1)	N(1)	Y	Y	Y	Y	N	Y	Y	Y

VII. Communications Functions

	Software Package									
	ACT 2.11A	ACT for Windows	BIZ BASE 3.0	EMIS II 3.0	GOLD MINE 3.0	MARKET FORCE+ 5.0	PACK RAT—Windows	SNAP—windows	TELEMAGIC 3.0	TOTAL MANAGER 3.0
Remote update to central database—overwrite	Y	Y	Y	Y	N	N	Y	N	Y	Y
—Update if changed since last communication	Y	Y	Y(5)	Y	Y	Y	N	Y	3P	Y
Direct link with remote users	Y	Y	Y	Y	Y	Y	N	Y	Y	Y
Hot Key interface to other programs	Y	YW	YW	Y(1)	Y(1)	Y(6)	YW	YW	3P	YW
Fax interface	Y	N	Y	N	Y	Y	Y	Y	3P	Y
Automatic dial	Y	Y	Y	Y	Y	Y	Y	N(5)	Y	Y

Notes

ACT V. 2.11A + ACT for Windows

(1)   Software allows for ability to forward uncompleted items, but is cumbersome.

Biz Base

(1)   Electronic mail is available on the LAN version only.

(2)   Data dictionary is only available as a chart in the manual.

(3)   Sales projections are only available if you are using the quotation system.

(4) System has organizational structure that links records together; each record can have one additional contact, but can have unlimited records linked together.

(5) Notes are only mergable fields.

EMIS II

(1) Need to buy WordPerfect link; cost, $100.

(2) Has available a frequency distribution module that allows for reports to be calculated with percentages on any field.

(3) System has organizational structure that links records together; each record can have one additional contact, but can have unlimited records linked together.

(4) System brings up one activity on line at a time; does not show full screen of activity at one time.

(5) Can schedule unlimited items in calendar, but only one item can be linked to a record at a time.

GoldMine

(1) Link available only for Word Perfect 5.1.

(2) Several optional products of note:

— Lead source analysis reporting module

— Graphical and statistical analysis

Marketforce +

(1) Allows for order capture window, but not linked to any order processing or quotation system.

(2) Market plan management available through separate product—automated marketing system—not part of market force+ and is cumbersome to use.

(3) The security system is set up in control files and requires technical knowledge; is not easy to use.

(4) Available only by purchasing an additional product, the file conversion utility, for $249.

(5) Calls only are available on-line. Tasks do not come up on the screen.

(6) Hot key interface available for Macola, Platinum, and Great Plaines accounting software only.

PackRat

(1) Scheduled to be available fourth quarter 1993.

(2) Expense tracking includes checking accounts, accounts payable, and general ledger capability

(3) A project management and gant-charting system is available that tracks time. Call for details.

(4) Agenda by salesperson is available only with the LAN version of the software.

(5) Maintains calls, letters and tasks in separate files.

Snap

(1) A configuration tool kit is available that allows modifications to the database.

(2) 200 fields are available in each record. 14 records can be linked together to allow for up to 2,800 fields to be linked.

(3) System defaults to last contact used.

(4) Can set up system to begin at to-do list, which would show past-due items.

(5) Available in DOS product only, not Windows version.

TeleMagic

(1) Need TeleMagic control fields program to merge into word processor. Call for price.

(2) System does not handle quotations. You can enter and process orders. The system does not track revenue by account information.

(3) Electronic mail available in LAN version only.

(4) System can handle up to 999 user-defined fields, but they recommend no more than 250 for speed reasons.

(5) System has organizational structure that links records together; each record can have one additional contact, but can have unlimited records linked together.

(6) Agenda/calendar system is not integrated with the client record information. Only one recall field is available in the client record.

(7) Only recall field and notes information are tracked in the history file. None of the calendar activities are written to the history file or activity reports.

(8) Market plans can be set up using filters, macros, and user-defined fields but may be cumbersome.

Total Manager

(1) WordPerfect, Microsoft Word, and Ami Pro are the only product interfaces currently available for this program.

INDEX

A

Access, *see* System
Account(s), 31, 33, 73, 85, 94, 114
  see New
  information, 12
  management, 120
  profile, 9, 15
  record, 75
Accounts receivables, 21
Accuracy, 14
ACT for DOS, 171
ACT for Windows, 170
Action field, 55
Active customer, 121
Activity/activities
  see Activity-tracking, Multiple, Sales,
      Summary
  report(s), 115, 116
  reporting, 21, 50
  scheduling, 75
Activity-tracking functions, 159
Ad hoc
  report(s), 15, 123-124
    writer, 87
  reporting
    software, 123
    systems, 159
Administrative
  reports management, 20
  work, 115
Advertising, 26
Agenda, 78, 81
  follow-up management, 114
  functions, 44, 80
  management
    automation, 119
    capabilities, 10
    functions, 20, 54
    profile, 169, 187
    system, 76

reports, 15
schedules, 16
Appendix, 167-193
Appointments, 81
ASCII, 38, 108
Assets, 19
  computer management, 20-29
AT&T, 108, 112
Automated
  appointment systems, 80
  call
    backs, 113-114
    systems, 80
  contact management systems, 62
  follow-up systems, benefits, 61-63
  mailing, 20
  tickler system, 74-75
Automatic dialing, 86, 125
  menu, 86
Automation, 83
  see Sales automation, Sales process
  determination, 113-144
  objectives, 101-102

B

Back-up capability, 109
Bad debts, 21
Bankruptcy, 33
Big brother syndrome, 105
BIZ BASE GOLD, 172
Black hole syndrome, 78-80
Board of directors, 8
Booked orders report, 21
Branching responses, 125
Budget(s), 127, 153, 156, 160, 167
Budgetary process, 52
Bulk mailings, 51
Business
  asking, 121
  computer system, 32, 47

Customer(s), 14, 18, 23, 26, 42, 62, 91, 105
  attitudes, 64, 74
  contact, 116
  profile, *see* Ideal
  satisfaction, 63, 74
  service, 63, 64, 105
    calls, 64, 74
    contact management software use, 64-65
    levels, 15
    improvement, 116
    problem, 64
    representatives, 16, 89
    staff, 100, 114
Customized reporting, 14, 18

D

Data
  see Corrupted, Critical, History, Internal, Notes, Opportunity
  accuracy, 35
  communication, 95
    processes, 155
  conversion plan, 156
  corruption, 110
    see Corrupted
  entry
    accuracy, 35, 39
    fields, 106
  importing/exporting capabilities, 108-109
  input, 35, 83, 91
    pre-definition, 125-126
  management function, 169, 190-191
  manipulation, 87
  processing, *see* Internal
  security, *see* Security
Database, 8, 33, 34, 37, 70, 84-85, 92, 94
  see Contact, Corporate, Notes, Opportunity, Relational
  importation, 37-38
  inquiry, 10
  mass changes, 85-86
  reading, 124
Date conflict alarm, 75

Dealers, 91, 105
Decision makers, 22, 42, 66, 71
  see Prospect
Decision time frame, 71
Decision-making
  see Management
  abilities, 9
  process, 32, 47
Demographic(s), 56
  information, 10, 62, 119
Demonstrations, 47, 48, 121
  see Product
Developing Solution stage, 22, 26, 32, 48
DIF, 38
Direct mail, 13, 18, 26, 59, 116
  campaigns, 14, 62, 115
Discipline, 34, 164-165
Distributing businesses, 2
Distribution channels, 150
Distributors, 29, 31, 44, 85, 101-105
Dollar fields, 38, 169
DOS, 111, 112
  file structures, 38
  Hot Key, 111
Duplicate records, checking, 124

E

Earnings, 82
Effectiveness, 1, 2, 27
  see Marketing plan, Sales
Efficiency, 78, 83
Electronic
  mail, 15, 18
    programs, 64
  memos, 16
  notepads, 16
EMIS II, 173
Employees, 152
  number, 71
Enhancements, 147
Expense(s)
  reports, 21
  tracking, 124
Expertise, 165
Exporting, *see* Data